"This is the most compelling plea to restore preaching to its time-honored status that I have ever read. This book deserves to be read and reread to light the fire of passion and conviction for all who would publicly proclaim, 'Thus says the Lord.' "

Erwin Lutzer
Moody Church, Chicago

"This books brings together the wisdom and experience of a number of foremost preachers of the present day. If it is received as it ought to be, we may yet see a mighty change for good in the current spiritual scene. I hope it will be widely read."

Iain Murray
Banner of Truth Trust
Edinburgh, Scotland

"*Feed My Sheep* is not only a passionate plea for preaching, but also a thorough review of what constitutes good preaching. Every minister of God's Word will profit from prayerfully reading this book."

Jerry Bridges
author of
The Pursuit of Holiness
Colorado Springs, CO

"Here some of this generation's most skilled shepherds provide passionate explanations of the priority and power of preaching God's Word that is a feast for Christ's sheep."

Bryan Chapell
Covenant Theological Seminary
St. Louis, MO

"There are a lot of books on preaching today, but not many good ones—this one is good. The subjects covered (and the accents of the authors as well) commend this volume to the minister and seminary student—and, indeed, to the church member who wants to learn what a real preaching ministry looks like, and who wants that for his church and from his pastor. It is spiritually challenging and topically pertinent."

Ligon Duncan
First Presbyterian Church
Jackson, MS

"There has never been a greater need for good preaching, and this book will help. In it some of the best preachers I know share their passion for preaching biblical, practical, expositional sermons that inform the mind and touch the heart. *Feed My Sheep* will be a tremendous help to anyone learning to preach and will provide real refreshment for anyone in the gospel ministry."

Philip Graham Ryken,
Tenth Presbyterian Church
Philadelphia PA

"When I was in seminary, my homiletics professor encouraged us to set a lifetime goal of reading at least one book each year on preaching. If you can read only one book this year on preaching, make it *Feed My Sheep*. Students and experienced preachers alike can find both timely and timeless teaching here. *Feed My Sheep* is simply one of the best books on preaching to come along in years."

Don Whitney
author of *Spiritual Disciplines
for the Christian Life*
Kansas City, MO

Feed My Sheep

A Passionate Plea for Preaching

R. Albert Mohler, Jr.
James Montgomery Boice
Derek Thomas
Joel R. Beeke
R. C. Sproul
John H. Armstrong
Sinclair Ferguson
Don Kistler
Eric Alexander
John Piper
John MacArthur

Don Kistler, General Editor

Soli Deo Gloria Publications
. . . *for instruction in righteousness* . . .

Soli Deo Gloria Publications
A Division of Soli Deo Gloria Ministries, Inc.
P. O. Box 451, Morgan PA 15064
(412) 221-1901/FAX 221-1902
www.SDGbooks.com

1-57358-144-5

Several translations of the Bible are used by the various authors: Drs. Mohler and Piper used the updated New American Standard Bible. Dr. Kistler used the 1977 New American Standard Bible. Drs. Boice, Armstrong, and Ferguson, and Rev. Alexander used the New International Version. Drs. Thomas and Piper used the Revised Standard Version. Drs. Sproul and Beeke used the King James Version. Drs. Thomas and Ferguson used the English Standard Version.

Library of Congress Cataloging-in-Publication Data

Feed my sheep : a passionate plea for preaching / R. Albert
    Mohler, Jr. ... [et al.] ; Don Kistler, general editor.
    p. cm.
    ISBN 1-57358-144-5 (pbk. : alk. paper)
    1. Preaching. I. Mohler, R. Albert, 1959-   . II. Kistler,
Don.
    BV4211.3.F44 2002
    251--dc21

2002012754

To William Harris

lover of the Puritans,
lover of preaching,
and lover of Christ

The shepherd is asleep where the willows weep,
And the mount is filled with lost sheep.

Bob Dylan

Contents

Foreword

Another book on preaching perhaps calls for some explanation. If the names in the table of contents are not sufficient in themselves to answer any query as to "why," I suggest the following: preaching in the contemporary English speaking world—and even in the evangelical and Reformed community—has not been impervious to the negative forces brought to bear on proclamation as a method of evangelism and discipleship. Both a video-drowned and educationally-challenged culture, and a church bent on accommodating herself to the regnant communication theories of the day, challenge the minister committed to the "foolishness of preaching." There is significant pressure on the preacher to truncate and thin out his message, to entertain, to explore alternative media for the advancement of the gospel, and even to abandon historic modes of proclamation altogether. Such a milieu is discouraging in the extreme for the preacher (young or old, novice or master) who simply wants to be faithful. In such a setting, every encouragement is useful. Indeed, it helps to beat this old drum and remind men that they are not crazy for wanting to be faithful, to say to them, "Stay at the wheel; hold fast; keep on;

don't give up; you're not alone." For this reason alone, this book may prove to be a real comfort and inducement to servants of the Word.

The subjects covered (and the accents of the authors as well) commend this volume to the minister and seminary student—and, indeed, to the church member who wants to learn what a real preaching ministry looks like, and who wants that for his church and from his pastor. R. Albert Mohler, Jr. dares to implore the overstretched, multi-tasking modern technician and spiritual therapist called a "pastor" that his ministry must be so prioritized that the preaching of the Word becomes so central that everything else must fall into place behind this priority. Surely that is a timely exhortation, and a welcome, balancing emphasis to the siren calls of other lesser duties and congregational expectations.

James Boice helps buttress the preacher's resolve to stick with the "foolishness of preaching" in an age in which biblical authority is at a discount, and congregations want their ears tickled instead of their hearts and minds challenged and instructed.

Derek Thomas's piece on expository preaching is a gem, one of the best short treatments of this issue you'll ever read. He bravely tips over some contemporary sacred cows and manages to advocate ably for the plan of consecutive, expositional preaching (that is, preaching through Bible books)—surely a necessary emphasis in our time.

Joel R. Beeke makes a strong case for the classical Reformed view of ministerial piety and experiential preaching (a view which, it must be said, is out of step with many of the currents of present-day Reformed thought). A prayerful reading of that chapter may awaken us to the older, wiser counsel of our forefathers and bring a helpful corrective to the anti-experiential tendencies of our theological environment.

R. C. Sproul, in his usual engaging style, urges preachers to know the truth and teach it. He explores the possibilities of and problems in doing that, all the while drawing on the counsel of Martin Luther regarding the task of teaching the Word.

John Armstrong gives a call to a truth-driven gospel ministry. In his helpful chapter, he reminds us, in the mode of C. S. Lewis, that we must commend the gospel to people because it is true, not simply because it is good for them. The generations of today are not big on truth (especially the 40 and older crowd in evangelical churches), and so again Armstrong's points are well taken.

Sinclair Ferguson helpfully addresses the task of preaching to the heart. Reformed preachers aren't known for this in our day, but this was a hallmark of the older Reformed tradition, and

Sinclair Ferguson is himself a master of it. Lest one accidentally get the impression that this book's cry for substance in preaching is a call for arid information-conveyance, this chapter will put you right (of course, there are many calls for heart-preaching throughout this book).

Don Kistler urges men to preach with authority, with examples of biblical preachers who did so, not the least of whom was our Lord. This, too, is an important counter balance to the chatty, self-effacing, tentative, informal, dialogical banter that sometimes passes for preaching today.

Eric Alexander, one of the archetypal Reformed preachers of our time, provides us with a Pauline perspective on evangelistic preaching (for those who still harbor suspicions that Reformed evangelistic preaching is an oxymoron!).

John Piper's timely treatment of preaching to those who are in the seminary of suffering is simply brilliant. In his characteristic, God-exalting, grace-conveying manner, Piper deals with a subject of vital importance to the gospel ministry. There are broken hearts under our noses every time we preach, and that means we need a biblical grid for speaking to them. Piper gives this to us.

John MacArthur concludes the book by pointing us away from the messenger to the message preached, surely an important word of spiritual counsel in our success-focused and personality-centered culture. We are not the reason the gospel works; the gospel is the reason the gospel works.

This is a good book to read on preaching; it is spiritually challenging and topically pertinent. We find here an assemblage of veritable titans of robust evangelicalism, all of whom share in common a firm commitment to and ability for expository preaching (that is, the faithful explanation and application of the Bible in which the text of Scripture supplies the matter of the preacher's exhortations rather than the preacher using the text as an occasion for his own expostulations, however helpful they may be). Their topics are timely, their counsel is wise, and they will richly and quickly reward the teachable reader.

Dr. Ligon Duncan

- Senior Minister, First Presbyterian Church, Jackson MS
- Adjunct Professor, Reformed Theological Seminary
- Board Member, Soli Deo Gloria Ministries
- Council, Alliance of Confessing Evangelicals
- Executive Committee, Council on Biblical Manhood and Womanhood
- Convener, Twin Lakes Fellowship

Author Profiles

Dr. R. Albert Mohler, Jr. is the president of the Southern Baptist Theological Seminary in Louisville, Kentucky. He holds the M.Div. and Ph.D. degrees from Southern Seminary. He has appeared on such national television programs as *Larry King Live*, the *Today* show, and *Dateline NBC*. The *Chicago Tribune* has called him "an articulate voice for conservative Christianity at large." Dr. Mohler is an ordained Southern Baptist minister.

Dr. James Montgomery Boice (1938-2000) was pastor of the Tenth Presbyterian Church in Philadelphia, Pennsylvania, for over 32 years. He was a member of the International Council on Biblical Inerrancy and an editor for *Christianity Today*. Dr. Boice was a prolific author, and founded the Philadelphia Conference on Reformed Theology. In addition to his weekly preaching duties, he had an extensive radio ministry through his "Bible Study Hour" program.

Dr. Derek Thomas, originally from Wales, is Associate Professor of Systematic and Practical Theology as well as Dean of Chapel at Reformed Theological Seminary in Jackson, Mississippi. After pastoring for 17 years in Belfast, Northern Ireland, Dr. Thomas returned to the United States in 1996 where, in addition to his work at the seminary, he serves as the Minister of Teaching at First Presbyterian Church in Jackson. In addition to serving in the pastorate, Derek has served as editor of the *Evangelical Presbyterian*, a monthly denominational magazine. A graduate of RTS in 1978, he received a Ph.D. from the University of Wales, Lampeter, in Calvin's preaching on the book of Job. He has written numerous books, including *The Storm Breaks: Job Simply Explained*; *Wisdom: the Key to Living God's Way*; *God Strengthens: Ezekiel Simply Explained*, and most recently, *Making the Most of Your Devotional Life*, based on the Ascent Psalms, and *Praying the Savior's Way*, based on the Lord's Prayer. Several more books are to appear shortly, including *Let's Study Revelation*, a commentary on the book of Revelation, and *Incomprehensibilitas Dei: Calvin and the Book of Job*.

Dr. Joel R. Beeke is the pastor of Heritage Netherlands Reformed Congregation of Grand Rapids, Michigan, and President and Professor of Systematic Theology and Homiletics at Puritan Reformed Theological Seminary. He earned a Ph. D. in Reformation and Post-Reformation Theology from Westminster Theological Seminary in Philadelphia.

He is the author of numerous books, most recently *Bringing the Gospel to Covenant Children; Family Worship; Puritan Evangelism: A Biblical Approach; The Quest for Full Assurance: The Legacy of Calvin and His Successors; Truth that Frees: A Workbook on Reformed Doctrine for Young Adults;* and *Reformed Confessions Harmonized* (with Sinclair Ferguson). Several more books are to appear shortly, including *Let's Study the Epistles of John; Overcoming Worldliness; A Primer on Calvinism;* and *A Reader's Guide to Puritan Literature.* Dr. Beeke is also editor of *The Banner of Sovereign Grace Truth* magazine, editorial director of Reformation Heritage Books, and radio pastor for "The Gospel Trumpet." He was a contributing author to *Justification by Faith ALONE!, Sola Scriptura, Trust and Obey,* and *Onward Christian Soldiers.*

Dr. R. C. Sproul is founder and chairman of Ligonier Ministries in Orlando, Florida. He is an ordained minister in the Presbyterian Church of America, in addition to being Distinguished Visiting Professor of Systematic Theology and Apologetics at Knox Theological Seminary in Ft. Lauderdale, Florida. Dr. Sproul is in constant demand as a speaker and author. He has authored many books, among them *The Holiness of God, Chosen by God, Abortion: A Rational Look at an*

Emotional Issue, and *Knowing Scripture.* He was a contributing author to *Justification by Faith ALONE!, Sola Scriptura, Trust and Obey,* and *Onward Christian Soldiers!*

Dr. John Armstrong is the President of Reformation & Revival Ministries, located in Carol Stream, Illinois. He was a Baptist pastor for over twenty years before assuming his present position in 1992. He also serves as the editor of *Reformation & Revival Journal* and *Viewpoint,* while conducting an international itinerant speaking ministry. He is the general editor of *Roman Catholicism: Evangelical Protestants Analyze What Unites and Divides Us, The Coming Evangelical Crisis,* and *The Compromised Church.* He is the author of *True Revival,* and *The Stain That Stays.* Dr. Armstrong was also a contributing author to *Justification by Faith ALONE!, Sola Scriptura, Trust and Obey,* and *Onward Christian Soldiers!*

Dr. Sinclair Ferguson is pastor of St. Georges–Tron Parish Church in Glasgow, Scotland. He is a graduate of the University of Aberdeen in Scotland and holds both the M.A. and Ph.D. degrees from that institution. Since 1976 he has been assistant editor of the Banner of Truth Trust. Dr. Ferguson is the author of numerous books, among them *Taking the*

Christian Life Seriously, Know Your Christian Life, Grow in Grace, Discovering God's Will, A Heart for God, Kingdom Life in a Fallen World, and *Handle with Care.* Dr. Ferguson is ordained in the Church of Scotland and maintains a worldwide ministry, preaching and teaching in churches and conferences. He and his wife Dorothy have four children. He was a contributing author to *Sola Scriptura.*

Dr. Don Kistler is the founder and president of Soli Deo Gloria Ministries, Inc. He received the M.Div. degree from Luther Rice Seminary in Jacksonville, Florida, and the D.Min. degree from Whitfield Theological Seminary in Lakeland, Florida. He is the author of *A Spectacle Unto God: The Life and Death of Christopher Love* and *Why Read the Puritans Today?* He is also the editor of all the Puritan reprints published by Soli Deo Gloria, and was a contributing author to *Onward Christian Soldiers.*

Rev. Eric Alexander is the former pastor at St. George's–Tron Parish Church in Glasgow, Scotland. He is in great demand as a speaker, and has spoken for the Ligonier Ministries Conference, the Philadelphia Conference on Reformed Theology, and the Soli Deo Gloria Conference, to name just a few.

Dr. John Piper is pastor of the Bethlehem Baptist Church in Minneapolis, Minnesota. He holds the B.Div. degree from Fuller Theological Seminary and a doctorate from the University of Munich. He taught biblical studies at Bethel College for six years before accepting his current pastorate. Dr. Piper is known through his Desiring God Ministries. He is the author of *God's Passion for His Glory: Living the Vision of Jonathan Edwards; Desiring God; The Legacy of Sovereign Joy*, and numerous other books.

Dr. John MacArthur, Jr. is pastor/teacher at Grace Community Church in Sun Valley, California. A graduate of Talbot Theological Seminary, he can be heard daily throughout the country on his radio program, *Grace To You*. He is the author of numerous bestsellers, including: *The Gospel According to Jesus, The Vanishing Conscience, Faith Works, Charismatic Chaos*, and his new book on discernment, *Reckless Faith*. Dr. MacArthur also serves as President of the Master's College and Seminary in Southern California. He was a contributing author to the Soli Deo Gloria volumes *Justification by Faith ALONE!, Sola Scriptura, Trust and Obey*, and *Onward Christian Soldiers!*

The Primacy of Preaching

R. Albert Mohler, Jr.

Evangelical pastors commonly state that biblical preaching is the hallmark of their calling. Nevertheless, a careful observer might come to a very different conclusion. The priority of preaching is simply not evident in far too many churches.

We must affirm with Martin Luther that the preaching of the Word is the first mark of the church. It is the first essential mark of the church. Luther believed so much in the centrality of preaching that he stated, "Now, wherever you hear or see this Word preached, believed, professed, and lived, do not doubt that the true *ecclesia sancta catholica* [Christian holy people] must be there . . . . And even if there were no other sign than this alone, it would still suffice to prove that a Christian, holy people must exist there, for God's Word cannot be without God's people and, conversely, God's people cannot be without God's Word."[1]

---

[1] Martin Luther, "On the Councils and the Church," in Luther's *Works* [*LW*], ed. Jaroslav Pelikan (vols. 1-30) and Helmut T. Lehmann (vols. 31-55), vol. 41, "Church and Ministry": III, ed. Eric W. Gritsch, trans. Charles M. Jacobs and Rev. Eric W. Gritsch (Philadelphia: Fortress Press, 1966), 150.

The preacher is called to be a servant of the Word. That is an expression of a very proud and glorious lineage in Christian history. But, as a title, it was particularly made well-known among preachers in 1941 when H. H. Farmer delivered his addresses on preaching and then published them under the title *The Servant of the Word*.[2]

In 1941, H. H. Farmer represented the neo-orthodox recovery of preaching. After a period of theological and homiletical sterility, figures such as Farmer in England, Barth in Switzerland, and others in the English speaking world and in greater Europe, sought to re-assert the case for preaching. In *The Servant of the Word*, Farmer actually had very little to say about the Word. He had a great deal to say about preaching, however. He argued for the assertion of the Christian message and the retention of preaching in the church. It is interesting, over six decades later, to go back to 1941 and see that a case was made for the retention of preaching. The neo-orthodox recovery of preaching was a house built on theological sand—it did not last.

In counterpoint, you can understand that what necessitated such an argument was the assertion, which must have been quite widespread at the

---

2 Herbert H. Farmer, *The Servant of the Word* (London: Nisbet and Co., 1941).

time, that preaching was simply an outmoded form of Christian communication. It was something the church could do without. Farmer maintained, however, that the practice of preaching was indispensable to Christianity. In so doing, Farmer wrote a great deal about the "I-Thou" relationship with a view to making preaching relevant. Looking back six decades later, however, we see that there was never much to Farmer's recovery.

Yet Farmer did get some things right. First, he argued for the unique power and preeminence of preaching in Christianity. The history of religion's approach was very influential at that time. These figures held that preaching was part of virtually every religious system in one way or another. Farmer maintained, however, that such a claim simply was not honest. Preaching has a priority among Christians that it does not have among others, and this is because of the very nature of the gospel.

He further argued that the unique authority of Christian preaching comes from the authority of revelation and, in particular, the Bible. Against those who maintained that revelation was basically internal, emotional, and relational, Farmer argued that it was given. Consider his following statement:

> For Christianity is a religion of revelation; its central message is a declaration, a proclamation that God has met the darkness of the human

> spirit with a great unveiling of succoring light
> and truth. The revelation moreover is histori-
> cal, that is to say, it is given primarily through
> events which in the first place can only be re-
> ported and affirmed. As we have already said,
> no merely internal reflection can arrive at his-
> torical events. If a man is to be saved, he must
> be confronted again and again with the given-
> ness of Christ.[3]

This is an interesting statement. Made back in
1941, we discover an argument for the retention of
preaching, an argument for the preeminence of
preaching in the Christian church, and an argument that Christian preaching is distinguished by
virtue of its grounding in revelation. It is the
preaching of a word that has been given; it is not
the invention of a message that has been devised.

My concern, of course, is not with what H. H.
Farmer thought about the preacher as the servant
of the Word. I want an apostolic authority, one inspired by the Holy Spirit, namely, the Apostle Paul.
I am concerned with what the great apostle
thought about preaching and how he understood
himself to be the servant of the Word. To do this I
want to examine Colossians 1:25–29:

> Of this church I was made a minister according

------

[3] *Ibid.*, 86.

to the stewardship from God bestowed on me for your benefit, so that I might fully carry out the preaching of the Word of God, that is, the mystery which has been hidden from the past ages and generations, but now has been manifested to His saints, to whom God willed to make known what is the riches of the glory of this mystery among the Gentiles, which is Christ in you, the hope of glory. We proclaim Him, admonishing every man and teaching every man with all wisdom, so that we might present every man complete in Christ. For this purpose also I labor, striving according to His power, which mightily works within me.

This is a majestic passage. The Apostle Paul, writing to the church at Colossae, speaks of his own understanding of the apostolic ministry, of his stewardship of the mysteries of God, and of his stewardship of the task of proclaiming the Word of God. He speaks of his calling, his message, and the purpose of his preaching. This is Paul's declaration of ministry. You notice in verse 24 that this explains why Paul submits to suffering. "Now I rejoice in my suffering for your sake, and in my flesh I do my share on behalf of His body, which is the church, in filling up what is lacking in Christ's afflictions."

Paul explains why he endures such suffering, and why he not only endures the suffering but, of all things, rejoices in these sufferings. This is gloriously counterintuitive. Why? Because these sufferings have earned him the opportunity for the preaching of the gospel, the preaching of the Word. He understands himself as a servant of the Word, and he sees his purpose on earth as one of preaching this Word and proclaiming Jesus Christ.

This passage does not represent superficial triumphalism, but genuine gospel triumph. It is a sober triumph because Paul acknowledges the sufferings he is currently enduring, but he also understands the victory that is assured in Christ. It is not Paul's triumph. It is Christ in Paul, the hope of glory.

In contrast, we look at the contemporary church. We notice the exhaustion of preaching that has taken place in so many pulpits. Rarely do we hear these days that a church is distinguished primarily by its preaching. When we hear persons speak about their own congregation, or when they make comparative remarks about other congregations, generally they speak about something other than preaching. They speak of its "ministry." They speak, perhaps, of its specialized ministry to senior adults, children, or young people. They speak of its music. They speak of its ministries of one sort or another. Sometimes they speak of things far more superficial than those. Or perhaps they speak of the church's Great Commission vigor and commitment—and for that we are certainly thankful. But rarely do you hear a church described, first and foremost, by the character, power, and content of its preaching.

I acknowledge that pastors have a certain "product envy." We envy those who build houses or sell cars or build great corporations or assemble automobiles, or merely those who cut the grass. Why? It is because they have something tangible to show for their labor at the end of the day. They may be fastening widgets and assembling automobiles, or they may be putting things in boxes and sealing them up and sending them out, or they may be cutting the grass. They can see the product of their hands. A carpenter or an artist or a building contractor has something to which he can point. But what about the preacher?

The preacher is robbed of that satisfaction. We are not given the sight to see what we would like to see. It seems like we stand up and throw out words and wonder, "What in the world becomes of them? What happens from it? What after all, is our product, and where in the world can you see it?" Words, words, and more words. We sometimes feel like we are flattering ourselves that people even remember what it was we had to say. We are chastened from even asking our own church members and fellow

believers for the identity of our text halfway
through the next week. Why? Because we are afraid
that we will get that shocked look of anticipated
response when a person of good intentions simply
says, "That was a fine message. I don't remember
exactly what it was about, and I have a very vague
recollection of something you may have said, but I
want you to know it was powerful."

The Apostle Paul responds to this, at least
somewhat, in verse 23 when he writes to the Colossians saying, [All of this is true,] "if indeed, you
continue in the faith firmly established and steadfast and not moved away from the hope of the
gospel that you have heard, which was proclaimed
in all creation under heaven and of which I, Paul,
was made a minister." Paul understood that it was
possible to hear in vain, and he hoped that it was
not true of this church, that their response to his
preaching was not just a succession of nice acco-
lades and respectful comments. Rather, we would
like to have an assembly line of maturing
Christians go out the door of the church, wherein
we could at least see something and note some
progress. We could statistically even mark what
kind of impact this sermon had over against another. But we do not have that sight; it is largely a
hidden work in the human heart. Such a work will
bear good fruit, but this will take time to be evident.

Since the Lord established His church, there have been preachers, lots of preachers. The church has heard good preachers and poor preachers, faithful preachers and faithless preachers, eloquent preachers and pulpit babblers, pulpit humorists and pulpit bawlers, expository preachers, narrative preachers, thematic preachers, evangelistic preachers, literary preachers, sawdust preachers, postmodern preachers, seeker-seeking preachers, famous preachers, infamous preachers—lots and lots of preachers. To what end? It all accumulated to millions and millions of hours preaching. You go all the way back to the first century and try to estimate how much time has been consumed in preaching, and we should measure not only the time of the preacher, but the time and attentiveness of the congregation as well.

This represents a massive investment of human time, energy, and attention in the task of preaching. For what? To what end? Millions and millions of hours of preaching, countless books, conferences, and controversies. So what? The preacher may sound like Luther on Sunday, but he feels like bathing in Ecclesiastes on Monday morning: "Vanity, vanity, all is vanity." Striving after the wind—that is what it feels like. We feel like the preacher of Ecclesiastes who laments in chapter 1:15, "What is crooked cannot be straightened and

what is lacking cannot be counted." Vanity. It is
such a deal to be called to preach. You work hard
and you often see nothing. This is not piece work,
it is just a piece of work, we feel so often.

Furthermore, this line of work has a nasty way
of getting you into trouble. It seems that the more
faithful one is in preaching, the more trouble one
encounters. Why? There is conflict and controversy.
You preach the Word. You did not come up with
it. This is not your opinion, and it is not something
you came up with in order to offend people. You
are simply preaching the Word. After all, that is
your assignment. So you preach the truth, and the
next thing you know you are on the front page of
the papers. You are the subject of gossip for the
deacons and their wives; even the youth group is
up in arms over whatever you said. Conflict and
controversy are always hard, and they again tend to
be correlated to faithfulness in preaching. The
harder you work at it, the greater the risk, the
higher the stakes. And it is not just conflict and
controversy. Sometimes, preachers have experienced persecution or even martyrdom.

The man who wrote this letter to the Colossians
was himself a martyr for the faith. In giving his final instructions to Timothy he speaks of being
poured out as a libation. He is ready to be offered
as an offering. The sufferings of which he speaks

in Colossians 1:24 are going to be realized in a martyrdom that is yet before him. There have been martyrs throughout the history of the church, such that the blood of the martyrs has been the seed of the church, the nourishment of the church. Moreover, the church is repeatedly persecuted. Do you not imagine that your preaching priorities would become self-evidently clear under persecution? After all, if you are forced to meet in a catacomb, and if as you gather together you know that at any time you might be arrested, you are going to weigh every word. There is not going to be any time for pulpit frivolity. There is not going to be any time to promote the next youth program. Everything is going to be concerned with getting down to the reality of the eternal Word of God.

But, sometimes preachers are ejected and fired. That is simply one of the realities of pulpit ministry. Sometimes it happens that preaching the Word is met with antipathy and resistance. Why? Because "the Word of God is living and active and sharper than any two-edged sword . . ." (Hebrews 4:12). And as the Lord spoke to His prophet Isaiah (55:11): "[My Word] will not return to Me empty, without accomplishing what I desire." Sometimes this means that God uses the Word to rebuke and correct His people. And it is the preacher who must speak that word and reap the response.

Indeed, I will go so far as to assert that if you are at peace with the world, you have abdicated your calling. You have become a court preacher to some earthly power, no matter how innocuous it may appear. To put it straight: you have been bought! If there is no controversy in your ministry, there is probably very little content to your preaching. The content of the Word of God is not only alive and active, it is sharper than any two-edged sword, and that means it does some surgery. It does some cutting, and that leads to bleeding, and by God's grace there then comes healing, and there is always controversy.

Paul is emphatically aware of the dynamic of which we are speaking. He understands the very real experience of preaching. He understands the frustration and sometimes he articulates it in his own words. Just read his letters. It is not as if he avoided the controversy. In 1 Corinthians 1:14 he laid it right before them, even to the point of saying, "I thank God that I baptized none of you except Crispus and Gaius." That's a rather strong word of correction. But this text hits us where we need it, because Paul not only endures all of this, he seems to revel in it, to celebrate it. Paul seems to understand all of the frustrations and the conflict and controversy and trouble of preaching, and yet he says, as it were, "Bring it on. This is what I was made for. This is what I was called to do. This is what I am here for. Let's get at it!"

In Colossians 1:24, he even rejoices in his sufferings for the sake of the church, for the body of Christ and for His glory. "Of this church," Paul says, "I was made a minister. I was not made a minister of some hypothetical, non-problematic, non-controversial church. I was made a minister of the church of the Lord Jesus Christ, of the body of Christ on earth, a chosen, purchased possession being sanctified even in the present, and struggling against the powers of sin and death and evil and darkness."

Paul makes the point in verse 25 that the central purpose of ministry is the preaching of the Word. In the end, everything comes down to this. "Of this church, I was made a minister according to the stewardship from God bestowed on me for your benefit, so that I might fully carry out *the preaching of the Word of God.*" In some translations, the words "the preaching of" are inserted there, and I believe that is a legitimate insertion. It is clear that what Paul means is that the carrying out the Word of God is achieved by the proclamation, the teaching, and the preaching of the Word of God. These are vivid terms. Paul speaks in such very strong language. He speaks here of the fact that he was made a minister. He did not make himself a minister anymore than he saved himself or appeared to himself on the Damascus Road. He was claimed, and as he was claimed, he was made a minister of the Word. In fact, he was made an apostle of the Lord Jesus Christ, and he understood his situation clearly. When he writes in 1 Corinthians 15:8, he explains that Christ appeared to him as "one untimely born." He called himself the "least of the apostles" in verse 9, because he had persecuted the church; but God's great triumphant sign of contradiction was in choosing the chief persecutor of the church to make him the apostle to the Gentiles.

Paul goes on to say that he has received this ministry according to the stewardship from God bestowed on him for the benefit of the Colossian church. I think this is very critical to the pastor's understanding of his calling and to the minister's understanding of the stewardship. We are assigned a stewardship from God which is bestowed on us not for our benefit, but for the benefit of the church. It is as if we have been drafted, called out, assigned, and granted a stewardship that we do not deserve, and a stewardship that we are not capable of achieving and fulfilling. Nonetheless, God chooses those instruments. In 1 Corinthians 1:20, 27–28, Paul wrote:

> Where is the wise man? Where is the scribe?
> Where is the debater of this age? Has not God
> made foolish the wisdom of the world? . . . God
> has chosen the foolish things of the world to
> shame the wise, and God has chosen the weak
> things of the world to shame the things which
> are strong, and the base things of the world
> and the despised God has chosen, the things
> that are not, so that He may nullify the things
> that are.

Why? It is thus apportioned so that, if there is any boasting, it has to be boasting in Him.

"We are stewards of the mysteries of God," Paul said, according to the stewardship God bestowed on him "for the benefit of the church." And why all of this? What is the bottom line? What is the essential point? The point, as you can see in the purpose clause of Colossians 1:25 is, "so that I might fully carry out the preaching of the Word of God." Paul's intention was not to dabble a little bit in preaching; nor was it his intention merely to add preaching to his ministerial resume or itinerary in order that he might complete himself as a well-rounded minister of the gospel. Nor was it that he would eventually get around to preaching in the midst of other pastoral responsibilities. No, he said, "All of this, in the end, is fulfilled and is only fulfilled, in the full carrying out of my responsibility of preaching the Word."

When the minister of the gospel faces the Lord God as judge, there will be many questions addressed to him. There will be many standards of accountability. There will be many criteria of judgment, but in the end the most essential criterion of judgment for the minister of God is, "Did you preach the Word? Did you fully carry out the ministry of the Word? In season and out of season, was the priority of ministry the preaching of the Word?"

This is not to say that there are not other issues, that there are not other responsibilities, or that there are not even other priorities; but there is one central, non-negotiable, immovable, essential priority, and that is the preaching of the Word of God. And Paul speaks to this so clearly when he states his purpose: "That I might fully carry out the preaching of the Word of God."

Contrast that with today's minister, and with today's congregational expectations. What we see is the marginalization of the pulpit. There is the recognition that "after all, it is an important piece of furniture in the sanctuary and someone ought to use it for something." Some would tell us, "Preaching has its place, but let's not let preaching get in the way of music, which is, after all, what draws people, and what establishes fellowship." Perhaps many of us could testify of going to a church service where something was said or even printed in the bulletin to the effect that "first we are going to have some praise and then we are going to get to preaching," or "first, we are going to have a time of worship and then we are going to turn to preaching." What do we think preaching is but the central act of Christian worship? As a matter of fact, everything else ought to build to the preaching of the Word, for that is when the God of whom we have been speaking and singing speaks to us from His eternal and perfect Word.

Contrast Paul's absolute priority with the congregational confusion of today's church. When you look at manuals, books, magazines, seminars, and conferences addressed to pastors, you notice that preaching, if included at all, is most often not the priority. When you hear people speak about how to grow a church, how to build a church, and how to build a great congregation, few and far between are those who say it comes essentially by the preaching of the Word. And we know why, because it comes by the preaching of the Word slowly; slowly, immeasurably, sometimes even invisibly, and hence we are back to our problem. If you want to see quick results, the preaching of the Word just might not be the way to go. If you are going to find results in terms of statistics, numbers, and visible response, it just might be that there are other mecha-

nisms, other programs, and other means that will
produce that faster. The question is whether it produces Christians.

Indeed, such techniques will not produce maturing and faithful believers in the Lord Jesus
Christ because that is going to come only by the
preaching of the Word. Preaching is not a mecha-
nism for communication that was developed by
preachers who needed something to do on Sunday.
It was not some kind of sociological or technologi-
cal adaptation by the church in the first century trying to come up with something to do between the
invocation and benediction. It was the central task
of preaching that framed their understanding of
worship, and not only their understanding of worship, but also their understanding of the church.

Luther was trying to go back to the first century
and understand the essential marks of the church,
and the first mark is preaching. Where the authentic preaching of the Word takes place, the church
is there. And where that is absent, there is no
church. No matter how high the steeple, no matter
how large the budget, no matter how impressive
the ministry, it is something else. Paul was determined fully to carry out his ministry of preaching
the Word of God, and he did so in the face of the
tyranny of the practical, the immediate, and the
seemingly productive, because his confidence, after

all, was in the Word of God.

The second essential issue found in this text is that the essential content of Christian preaching is the mystery of the gospel. "(T)hat is," Paul says in Colossians 1:26, "the preaching of the Word of God is seen in the mystery which has been hidden from the past ages and generations, but has now been manifested to His saints." A mystery? All around Asia Minor and the ancient world, at this time, were mystery religions and mystery cults, and there were some who thought, especially from the Roman perspective, that perhaps Christianity was just another one of these mystery cults. After all, it too had its mystery. And Paul said, "Guilty as charged, absolutely." Yet this is not a mystery of esoteric knowledge. This is not a gnosticism of elitist intellectuals. No, this is a mystery that was hidden by God until it could be publicly revealed in the incarnation of Jesus Christ, in His death, burial, and resurrection. This is a mystery! Go through the New Testament and see how many times the word "mystery" (*musterion*) appears. Obviously, there is something here to which we ought to give attention.

There is something deeply mysterious about Christian preaching, both in terms of its communication and in terms of content. For, after all, what we preach is not what the world expects to hear. It is not a message they will hear anywhere else. No

human wisdom, no school of philosophy, no secular salesman, no TV commercial speaker selling
his tapes, is ever going to come up with this, unless
it comes from the Word of God. If you look at what
is selling in the bookstores and you see who is selling the conferences, and you realize that if you can
tell people how to buy property, improve and sell it,
and make a million dollars, why, you could sell
your tapes. If you can tell people how they can lose
weight, you can sell just about anything. If you can
tell people how they can be handsome and wise,
have their children well-behaved and their pets like
them, you will find yourself a very popular speaker.
You could put your videotapes and audiotapes
together, and write books that will be sold in the
bookstores and hawked on television. But if you
preach the gospel, you just might discover that it is
not quite so popular. But it is powerful, and it is
mysterious. Why? Because it was a mystery that
God hid from previous generations in order that it
might be displayed publicly at the time of the Lord
Jesus Christ.

Look at Paul's statement in verses 26–27: "that
is, the mystery which has been hidden from past
ages and generations, but has now been manifested
to His saints, to whom God willed to make known
what is the riches of the glory of this mystery
among the Gentiles, which is Christ in you, the

hope of glory." As Paul quite personally knew, true preaching often leads to a riot. But the true preaching of the gospel is the preaching of the mystery of God. It is a *musterion*. It was hidden, but now it is revealed to the Gentiles. For the Gentiles had been understanding God's way about as correctly as someone using a Ouija board to try to understand the ways and the will of God. But now, out of that darkness, out of that confusion, out of that sinful depravity, out of that backwardness, and out of that ignorance comes the shining light of the gospel which is a mystery. It is the mystery of mysteries: Christ in us, the hope of glory.

There is glory, and there is a glory that can even come to us, but it is not ours. There is a glory we should seek, but it is not glory for ourselves, not to ourselves, but the glory of Christ. And that glory is most evident not just when Christ is preached as an abstract and objective truth, but when Christ becomes in us the hope of glory. Paul's concern was not just that his hearers would come to a correct cognitive understanding of the gospel, although that was essential. His concern was that the gospel would be received by faith and that lives would be transformed. Paul's wonderfully symphonic presentation of the gospel in the book of Romans helps us to understand how sinners become saints, how we are justified by faith, and how we are adopted as sons and daughters of the Most High God.

Paul understands this to be a mystery. And if it is a mystery for the Jews, it is even more a mystery for the Gentiles. Indeed, in those central passages in Romans, Paul helps to explain how it is that the branch of the wild olive tree has been grafted onto Israel. It is a mystery, and if you do not get excited about preaching this, I do not know what will excite you! The gospel is simply the most transformative, the most powerful, and the most explosive message there is. If you have a problem finding something to preach, I guarantee that you are not preaching the gospel.

"Christ in you, the hope of glory." This is explosive. It is controversial and transforming. The gospel, according to the Apostle Paul, is not simply offered to us on a platter for our convenience, our investigation, or our tasting. It is thrown at us like hot, blazing rocks, spewing forth from the crater of a volcano. It is uniquely dangerous. Our task is to preach the Word and to make known the mystery. But, making known the mystery requires diligence—painstaking, systematic, rigorous, expository preaching. Why? Because we have to paint the entire canvas.

Too many preachers are working out of one little corner of the great canvas of the work of God. Here is the plan of God throughout the ages, and they are specialists, perhaps, in this little corner. There are some preachers who, as painters, only have certain colors. Some have the vivid colors. Some have the subdued colors. But, in order to get the entire picture out there, what is required is rigorous expository preaching because we have to connect the dots.

We have to paint the whole picture and this means we have to go into the Old and New Testaments, and we have to use the analogy of faith, that is, the analogy of Scripture to interpret and apply Scripture by Scripture. We have to build upon knowledge so that the people of God are continually increasing in the knowledge of the Word of God, and that the Word of God is taking root in them and growing in them. And then they begin to see the whole picture. They understand its component parts; they understand the bright colors; and they also understand the subdued hues. Indeed, they understand the gospel. The mystery comes into focus, and that is the power of preaching. It's not going to come by any other means. Sadly, the doctrinal ignorance in the pulpits of today is being replicated in the doctrinal ignorance and indifference of the pews, and the people are not even seeing the picture, much less getting it.

What does it mean to be a servant of the Word? It means that the promise of true preaching is to present every Christian complete in Christ. How is that for a job description? This responsibility, should you choose to accept it, is that, at the end of your ministry, you be able to present Christians complete in Christ. Paul says this in verses 28–29: "We proclaim Him, admonishing every man and teaching every man with all wisdom, so that we may present every man complete in Christ. For this purpose also I labor, striving according to His power, which mightily works within me." That is a challenge!

Note again what Paul says here. "We proclaim *Him*." We preach Christ; we proclaim Him; we focus our message on Christ. We show Christ, the mystery of the ages, revealed in Scripture in the Old Testament and in the New. We proclaim Him from every opportunity and from every text. The best exhortation I know concerning this practice comes from the great Baptist preacher, Charles Spurgeon, who, in speaking to his students about expository preaching, told them to preach the text as the text and, as soon as possible, you make a beeline to the cross and show its fulfillment in Jesus Christ.

We preach Christ as a three-step process: first, proclaiming Christ, second, admonishing every man, and third, teaching every man. This issue of admonishing comes rather difficultly in our day, seen in the fact that there is precious little admonishing going on. Paul, however, believed in admonishing. In fact, he described his ministry in many ways as admonishing. He spoke of his ministry to the Ephesians, about staying there, admonishing them for a period of years.

What does it mean to admonish? For one thing, it means to get in the face. These days, with our ideal of personal autonomy and personal privacy, we, as Americans, feel that no one has the right to tell us what to believe, how to act, or what we must correct in terms of behavior or patterns of thought and life. After all, we reason, "Our marriages are our marriages. We are free to make and to break them. Our vocation is simply a matter between us and our employer. God does not have anything to do with it, and the church certainly better not stick its nose into it."

That is hardly the pattern in the New Testament, however. With a pattern of authentic Christian preaching, the Word is applied. I do not mean that it is applied in the sense that the preacher tries to find some way to make the text relevant. Rather, it is applied in that the text must be directly addressed to persons in the congregation: "This is what you must do. This is what you must be."

Isaac Backus, the great Baptist, was first an ex-

horter before he was a preacher. In revolutionary
America, the exhorter had a particular task in the
congregation, and this one was not likely to be
popular. After the preacher had preached, it was
his responsibility to apply the message. This might
mean going up to somebody and saying, "This is
going to be how you change your behavior." Now
Backus was 15 years old when he took on this assignment. So you had a 15-year-old (who was
probably expendable), and he would come up after
the preaching and say, "Now, Widow Jones, this
means you are going to have to change the way you
raise your children. And this means, Mr. Smith,
that you are going to have to change the way you
do your business. This means we are going to have
to be accountable to the Word of God, and we are
going to have to be accountable together."

Whether from the preacher or from the pulpit,
there simply is not much admonishment going on
in today's church. In our day, this would be seen as
intolerant and invasive and an imposition. Indeed,
it would be seen as arrogant. But the role of the
preacher is to expose error and to reveal sin. The
Word of God will do that, I promise you, because it
will be unavoidable as you preach the Word. It is
simply there in the text. We are going to have to
come into alignment with this text in terms of the
way we think, the way we worship, and the way we

live, or we are going to disobey. Those are the only options.

In 2 Timothy 3:16–17, Paul told Timothy that in the preaching of the Word he is to rebuke and to correct. This business of correcting is not very politically correct. Why? Because you have to say that someone is wrong, and that an understanding is wrong and needs to be brought into alignment with God's Word. It means the behavior needs to be rebuked. Sadly, the failure of church discipline in our age has led to the fact that the church is simply one voluntary association with a steeple alongside other voluntary associations in far too many cases.

The first task is proclamation; the second is admonishment; the third is teaching every man, specifically, the positive teaching of the Word of God with application. This is something that cannot be sequestered to Sunday School. We cannot assume that the teaching ministry of the church is fulfilled when you have a good children's education system. The teaching of the Word of God should be cross-generational. The teaching of the Word of God is to be progressive and accumulative, thereby growing saints toward maturity in the Lord Jesus Christ. Furthermore, the teaching of the Word of God is to comfort, and it should do so, foremost, from the pulpit, for the pastor is, of all things, the teacher of the church.

Teaching assumes authority. After all, we have to know what it is we are to teach. Far too many preachers think this is an authority that is personal. "It is my authority, for I am the one who has been elected to teach," or so the thought often goes. Others think that it is the authority of modern knowledge they bring in, or the authority of secular consensus that is needed. But there is only one authority that is the preacher's authority, and there is only one authority that undergirds and justifies his teaching ministry, and that is the authority of the Word of God. This Word is inerrant, infallible, authoritative, and trustworthy. It is that Word, and that Word alone, that is our authority; and it is not only the foundation, but the substance, the content of our teaching and preaching. In too many churches today there is an uncertain sound from the pulpit, a multiple choice of curriculum of doctrine being offered. We have our own version of "values clarification," but that is not the model of the Apostle Paul. It was not his understanding of his stewardship; nor is it the nature of our calling.

The awesome power of authentic preaching is seen in the fact that God uses preaching to present His saints complete in Christ. How are Christians going to grow? How are they going to be matured? How is the process of Holy Spirit-directed sanctification going to be seen in them? It is going to occur by the preaching of the Word. The preaching of the Word is made visible. Our product-envy is very temporary. For when we get to glory we are going to see the product of our preaching. We are going to see the fact that there are saints clothed in the righteousness of Christ. We are going to see men and women, brothers and sisters in Christ, made complete in Him, and that is our task. When we measure whether or not we are successful, it must be by this criterion, namely, are we seeing the saints growing to completeness in Jesus Christ?

Paul concludes by stating in verse 29 that it is for this purpose that he struggles, a struggle not in his own strength, but according to Christ's power which works mightily within us. The Apostle Paul knew that he was not up to this, but Christ is. His authority was nothing, but Christ is all-sufficient, as seen in His Word. This means we have to devote ourselves to preaching not as one priority among others, but as our central and highest priority.

What does it mean to be a servant of the Word? It means first, that our ministry is so prioritized that the preaching of the Word becomes so central that everything else must fall into place behind this priority—everything else. Are there other important tasks of ministry? Of course. Are there other important priorities of the church? Of course. But your personal schedule will reveal the priority of preaching, and your personal schedule will reveal just how serious you are about preaching. You find out quickly what a church believes about preaching by looking at its calendar and added expectations, and you find out what a preacher believes about preaching by looking at his calendar and his schedule.

Second, if we are genuinely servants of the Word, it means that our congregations are aware of this priority and honor it. The congregation needs to understand that preaching is not merely the preacher's responsibility; it is the congregation's responsibility. It is the congregation's responsibility to see that it is fed. It is the congregation's responsibility to see to it that it calls a preacher who will preach the Word. Then, it is the congregation's responsibility to hold him accountable for that preaching and to measure his effectiveness and his faithfulness to, of all things, the pulpit ministry.

Third, it means that if we are to be servants of the Word, our preaching must be truly expository. That is, it truly expounds and applies the text of Scripture, declaring the Word of God to the people of God and trusting the Holy Spirit to apply that Word. Be reminded that this kind of preaching can get a man into serious trouble, and the lack of this trouble ought to be a signal that, perhaps, this kind of preaching is not found in his pulpit.

Indeed, preaching the Word of God just might get you into hot water. But the preaching of the Word of God is the criteria, priority, and measure of ministry. It takes rigorous exposition, by which I do not mean just choosing texts we like, the texts we think will preach, or the text that will fall on all the right ears, but the text as it stands. I believe in verse by verse exposition, because otherwise we would never get to some of those angular texts that are just so difficult to preach. But they too are the inerrant, infallible, and authoritative Word of God. They are profitable for our preaching and for our teaching, and that is a measure of our stewardship.

Fourth, if we are servants of the Word, it will be evident that every other task and priority is submitted to that first priority task—the preaching of the Word—with the promise that it will balance all the others. For a ministry established in the preaching of the Word of God is going to be an evangelistic ministry. It cannot be otherwise. And a ministry that is established in the preaching of the Word of God is going to be a Great Commission ministry, for it could not be otherwise. Everything comes into proper balance because we do not have to worry about balancing a schedule, balancing a budget, or balancing priorities when we understand that the Word of God will establish those priorities. Then everything else will become clear.

In the final analysis, we will only know how faithful we have been in glory. Then, when we see our Savior face to face, and when we see all the saints to whom we have preached, we will discover whether or not our preaching contributed to their completeness in Christ. Paul said that all of this— the suffering, the diligence, the hard work, the controversy, and the martyrdom—was work for the glory of preaching the gospel. And he said the purpose is to see every man, every Christian, perfected in Christ, completed in Christ, and presented to our Lord and Savior. Failure at this task is simply too awful to contemplate.

The Foolishness of Preaching

James Montgomery Boice

I once asked a number of people which verses came to their mind when they thought about preaching. I had already gone to one of the concordances and looked up verses where the English words "preaching," "preacher," or "preach" occur, and I found that, even in these cases, which do not reflect all occurrences of the Greek and Hebrew root words (these are also translated "proclaim," "make known," "speak," and so on), there are 150 verses. So I began to ask people, "What verse most comes to your mind when you think of preaching?" Again and again people referred to 1 Corinthians 1:21, where it says, "God was pleased through the foolishness of what was preached to save those who believe."

I think that says something about the way many people regard what they hear coming from the pulpit. They think of it as foolishness. In the minds of many the content of preaching, and perhaps even the delivery of the sermon itself, is a very foolish thing.

Is preaching really foolish? It obviously is in some sense because Paul speaks about it in those words. Indeed, preachers will often say that there are times when they feel foolish as they try to bring a word from God to those living in the midst of a secular culture. Yet when we look at the passage from which that phrase comes, it is perfectly evident, even on a very superficial reading, that the apostle is using this word "foolishness" in a specialized sense. He is talking about that which is foolish in the world's eyes, but which in actuality is the wisdom of God unto salvation.

He does it in a very interesting context. For in this passage he speaks not only of foolishness and wisdom, but also of weakness and power (a parallel contrast) and signs versus what we would probably call the foundation stone of revealed religion.

Paul was one of those rare individuals who moved quite easily among diverse cultures. He was a Jew, but he had grown up in a Roman town and was greatly influenced by Greek culture. So he moved equally well within a Jewish community, a Greek community, and a Roman community. Everywhere he went he preached Christ. He found that he did not have exactly the same problem when he moved among the Greeks as when he moved among the Romans, or when he moved among Romans as when he moved among the

Jews. Each of these cultures had its own particular difficulty where the gospel was concerned.

The Roman difficulty was that they were proud of their power. They were the ones who ruled the world. It was their legions that held the barbarians at bay. It was their naval power that had brought order to the Mediterranean. It was their soldiers who kept the roads open and the brigands in their place. They controlled the greatest empire the world had ever seen. They were proud of their power. When the apostle spoke to the Romans in the context of a Roman culture, it was natural that the Jesus he preached (crucified under a Roman governor) seemed the epitome of weakness. What Paul had to show as he spoke to the Romans with their great concern for power is that, although Jesus is in a sense the weakness of God, this weakness of God is actually a power able to transform men and women. In Romans he says, "The gospel . . . is the power of God for the salvation of everyone who believes" (Romans 1.16).

With Jews the situation was not the same. If the Roman mentality was that of a military man who believes that the most important thing is strength, the Jewish mentality was what we might compare to the cults of our day. That is, the Jews wanted a sign; they wanted visible demonstrations. That is why they were always asking Jesus for miracles.

They did not like the signs He gave because they did not like Him, just as people today do not like the words of the Bible because they do not like the Bible's God. They say, "If only God would say something; if only God would speak to me." But God has spoken. The reason they do not accept it is that they do not like Him.

In the same way, the Jews were asking for miracles. To Jews, Jesus was a stumbling block. Paul maintained that far from being a stumbling block, though it seemed to be that to Jewish culture, the gospel of Christ was actually a foundation, a block over which one could stumble but which was actually the foundation stone of revealed religion.

This is the context in which Paul talks about foolishness. Only here, writing to Corinth, he has a Greek mentality in mind. Greece had lost the power it once had under Philip of Macedon and Alexander the Great. That dominion was gone. But what the Greeks did have (and the Romans did not, at least to the same degree) was wisdom. Greece produced the great philosophers. Greece provided the teachers. In most wealthy Roman homes, there was a slave who was responsible for the education of the children, and nine times out of ten he was a Greek. The Greeks were proud of this wisdom. When the early ambassadors of the gospel came, proclaiming that the ineffable God had become man in human flesh in order to die for our salvation, that contradicted everything the Greeks understood about philosophy. The basic principle of their philosophy was that mind is separated from matter, that spirit is separated from flesh. It was inconceivable to the Greek that there could be an incarnation. So what happened when Paul preached in Athens? They laughed, because his message seemed foolish. What Paul had to say to the Greeks was that this which appears to be foolishness, and is communicated in a manner which is conceived to be the height of folly, is actually the wisdom of God.

On the basis of 1 Corinthians 1:21, we can say that preaching is that wise means of God by which the wisdom of the world is shown to be foolishness, and the folly of the gospel, as the world conceives it, is shown to be true wisdom.

Grace in Conversions

Why is preaching so important? It obviously is. If you look over the whole of the Bible and ask which of the characters in the Bible were preachers, you'll find that nearly all were. There were exceptions, of course. But you'll find that most of the Bible's male characters fall into this category. The New Testament looks back to Noah and calls him a preacher of righteousness. Enoch is declared to be a preacher. Martin Luther thought that all the antedeluvians going right back to Adam were preachers. The prophets were preachers. So were many kings. The apostles and the apostles' disciples, people like Timothy, Titus, John Mark, Silas and others, were preachers. Preaching is obviously important in the biblical revelation. But the question is, "Why? Why is preaching so important as a means of grace?"

The obvious answer is that preaching is a means of conversion. It is by the preaching of the Word that God moves in the hearts and lives of people to turn them from sin to Jesus Christ. In Romans 10:14–15 Paul writes along these lines: "How, then, can they call on the one they have not believed in? And how can they believe in the one of whom they have not heard? And how can they hear without someone preaching to them? And how can they preach unless they are sent?"

This is one of those great theological chains of the apostle Paul. A few pages earlier in Romans there occurs perhaps the best known of these chains: "Those God foreknew He also predestined to be conformed to the likeness of His Son. . . . Those He predestined, He also called; those He called, He also justified; those He justified, He also glorified" (Romans 8:29–30). There you have an ascending chain beginning with the foreknowledge of

God and proceeding through predestination, effectual calling, justification and glorification. That is
the way Paul's mind operated. Here in Romans 10
we find the same thing. Only now he does not trace
the chain forward, as it were—that is, from where
we are now (or from the past) to where we are go
ing to be in the future—but rather backward. He
says, "Here are people who believe. Let's trace this
back and see what the origins of that belief were."
So he goes back from calling upon the name of
Christ to believing on the name of Christ, to hearing the name of Christ, to preaching, and the fact
that preachers are sent out by God.

Calling upon Christ corresponds to that moment of personal commitment in which we speak
to God in prayer saying, "Yes, I understand these
things and I do believe that Jesus died on the cross
not just to be a Savior, but to be my Savior. Now I
promise to follow him as my Savior and Lord."
That is calling upon Christ.

But Paul says, "Even before that there is this
matter of belief. No one calls on Christ until he or
she first believes on Him. This concerns the content
in the gospel. Faith is more than an intellectual as-
sent to certain things. Faith has several elements. It
has content or knowledge. It has the warming of
the heart, personal response. It has a volitional element or commitment. All are important, but at the

beginning is this matter of content. People have to know Him on whom they are to call, because no one can call on Christ for salvation who does not understand who He is and what He has done.

But how are they to understand? Paul answers, "They have to hear." How can they believe unless they hear about Christ?

Then he says, "And how are they to hear?" Obviously, the way they are to hear is by preaching. Someone has to go and let this message of salvation, centered in the Lord Jesus Christ, be known to them. This is the way of conversion, because what God does in preaching is take His Word, which is not the mere word of men but the Word of God, and use it in a supernatural way to create spiritual life within the heart of the one listening.

I think the verse that is most helpful in explaining what happens in the matter of regeneration is 1 Peter 1:23. Peter is speaking there of how we are born again: "You have been born again, not of perishable seed, but of imperishable, through the living and enduring Word of God." When Peter says that you are born again of imperishable seed, I do not believe that he is talking about the kind of seed you plant in the ground. That image is used elsewhere. It is used especially of the resurrection: the seed is planted in the ground, it dies, it rises again. But that is not what Peter is talking about in this text. He is using the word "seed" to mean the male element in human procreation. He is talking about new birth, and therefore illustrates this spiritual birth with physical birth. He says we are born again spiritually in a way that is analogous to how we are born first of all in a physical sense.

What is necessary to have a new life come into being? You have to have the sperm of the father and the egg or ovum of the mother. They have to come together. Peter is saying that this is what happens in the new birth. God first of all plants the ovum of saving faith in the heart of the man or woman, because even faith is not from ourselves; it is the gift of God, not by works, so that no one can boast. Then God takes His living Word, the seed of spiritual procreation, and allows that Word to be proclaimed in such a way that it goes into the person through the gate of the ears, through hearing, and penetrates the ovum of faith. As a result there is a spiritual conception; there is new life.

This life begins to grow within, and just as in the case of pregnancy there is a period when a woman is not even aware that she is pregnant, so there can be the same thing spiritually. The life is there but the person does not yet know what has happened. Things are beginning to change. The person is beginning to have an interest in spiritual things. He finds himself hungering for the Word of

God. He reads it. He begins to feed upon it. Then, as the months go by (sometimes longer and sometimes shorter), there is the point in a service when someone may say, "If you want to receive Jesus as your Savior, put up your hand," and so he puts up his hand and comes forward and the counselor says, "Well, now you're born again." That is indeed how it may seem, but actually he was alive when the Word did its work. It is just that now the birth has taken place.

This is what makes preaching so exciting! The best day of the week for me is Sunday. It is also the hardest day of the week. The thing that makes it the best is that I never know what is going to happen. I come to church. I do not know who is going to be there. I preach. I do not know all the problems of the people I am preaching to. I know some of them. I try to be as sensitive as I can, but the deep things in the heart one generally does not know. People sit and listen, each with his or her own problems, all at their own particular point along a line of spiritual pilgrimage. God takes the Word that is preached and speaks it to the heart, and afterward somebody will come up and say, "I don't know how you knew it, but what you said was exactly the thing I needed to hear. How did you know it? Did somebody tell you about me? Somebody must have."

I have had people get angry about that and say, "So-and-so told you about me and you were preaching at me." I did not even know who they were, but the Holy Spirit has a way of applying the Word forcefully. That is the way He brings about conversions.

One of my predecessors at Tenth Presbyterian Church, Donald Grey Barnhouse, used to say that when he preached to an audience he used to think of them as a lot of barrels sitting there on the pew. Most of them were empty. Some of them had gunpowder inside, and his job was to produce explosions. The way he did it was by striking the matches of the Word and throwing them into the barrels. When he hit one that had gunpowder there would be an explosion. God put the gunpowder there. Then, as the Word was preached, there was a spiritual ignition or rebirth. This is one of the reasons we should value preaching so highly.

Preaching is important as a means of grace not merely because it is used of God to bring about conversions, but also because it is used for our sanctification, that is, our growth in holiness once we are born again. If you look back in your life and ask what is it that God has most used in your life to make you grow, you will find that in the vast majority of cases it is preaching. I know that to be true in my own life. It is not that other elements

were not present. I had the sacraments, Christian
literature, others praying for me, fellowship groups,
all those things. But the thing that God used most
for my growth was the faithful exposition of the
Word. That Word got hold of me so that years
later, when I would hear something different, even
though I would on occasion have preferred to believe something else, I could not do it because I
knew it was not true. The preaching of the Word
that I had heard in my earlier days held me and
led me as God continued the work which He had
begun so many years before.

Preaching is also the primary means of growth
for the local church. There is a great deal of debate
about this in our day, but it is the preaching of the
Word that God most uses to build up a church, not
only numerically but above all (and far more im-
portantly) in the spiritual depth and understanding of the people who make up the congregation.

When we talk about the importance of preaching, preachers are inclined (modestly) to say, "Well,
after all, no one is indispensable." And, of course,
that is true, if you understand it in the right way.
But it is also false if you understand it in the wrong
way. It is true that God does not need us. God does
not need us to glorify Him. God does not need us
to worship Him. God does not need us to proclaim
the gospel. If the people at the time of Christ's entry

into Jerusalem had failed to cry out, Jesus said the stones would have cried out. God is well able to raise up preachers from the stones. But at the same time it is also true that if God has called a man to be a preacher in a particular situation, that man is, by the calling and disposition of God, indispensable for that situation. If he gives good leadership and provides good teaching from the Word, that church will go forward. If he fails to do it, that church will not go forward. It is not overstating the situation to say that this is true.

Many things are talked about as necessary for the health and growth of the church today. People talk about certain programs being essential. They are important. We have such a diversified culture that people have their own individual problems; the family is fragmented, and the kind of reinforcement along Christian lines that ought to take place in homes does not always take place. The church is trying to minister specifically at that point. Still, if you think back historically, say, to the time of the Great Awakening in this country, you will realize that at that time the churches had hardly any programs at all, at least nothing that we would recognize as programs. There were no youth groups, no graded Sunday schools, no bowling leagues, no baseball teams. But those churches were healthy. Why? Because they had the faithful preaching of the Word.

Do you know what is said to be the single most important factor for the growth of a church in California? The size of the parking lot! If you have a big parking lot, your church becomes a big church. So what you have to do, you see, is to get as much land as you can right off the bat.

But what is essential? It is the preaching and teaching of the Word of God, because as that is done God the Holy Spirit speaks through that Word to the hearts of Christian people (and unbelievers too) and provides not only the numbers but the kind of leadership in character and commitment that is necessary if a church is to go forward. When that happens, you can change all sorts of things. You can be deprived of a lot, but the body, which is the true church, is there and grows.

I do not think it is too much to say that preaching really is an essential means, perhaps even the most important means, of grace. If that is the case, then we should be very careful in our Christian life to expose ourselves to the best teaching and attend the best churches available.

What Kind of Preachers?

What kind of preachers do we need? If you are choosing a church, you want to look for the right kind of preacher. If you are on pulpit committees, you will be responsible for knowing how to look.

First, we need preachers who are born again. It should not be necessary to say that; it is self-evident. Yet it is necessary to say it because so many preachers are not born again. There are men standing in prominent pulpits of this land, thousands of pulpits, who are not regenerate.

Probably the second most influential sermon that has ever been preached on the North American continent was on this theme. The most important and most significant sermon very likely was Jonathan Edwards's "Sinners in the Hands of an Angry God" (included in the Soli Deo Gloria publication *The Wrath of Almighty God*). Number two was preached about the same time. As a matter of fact, it was preached in 1740, one year earlier than Jonathan Edwards's sermon, and was entitled "The Dangers of an Unconverted Ministry" (included in the Soli Deo Gloria reprint *Sermons of the Log College*). The preacher was Gilbert Tennent. He said, "Look into the congregations of unconverted ministers and see what a sad security reigns there, not a soul convinced [that is, converted] that can be heard of for many years together, and yet the ministers are easy because they say they do their duty. These caterpillars labor to devour every green thing and the chief object is not to preach the new birth but to keep the people in their interest." Then he said, "Natural men [that is, unconverted men] have no call of God to the ministerial work. So if a godly man finds himself in a church or denomination in which such natural men hold rule, then it is both lawful and expedient to go from there to hear godly persons."

You can imagine that Tennent got many preachers angry. But he told the truth, not only for his day but for ours as well. It is a sad thing that many preachers in our day are unconverted. Yet that is the first essential of true preaching.

Second, those who would be the kind of preachers God would use and whose preaching would be a means of grace must believe the Bible. The Bible is where God speaks, and it is the preacher's primary task—not his whole task, but his primary task—to exposit that Word.

I have had occasion to speak on this subject in many different places, and I find as I share some of my experiences and the things I have heard that lay audiences in particular are astounded to be told that so many ministers really do not believe the Bible. Yet that is the case. Ministers are somewhat reluctant to say what they really believe because, if they do, their congregations are likely to get rid of them. They will be out looking for another job. But they do say what they believe in the company of other ministers.

I was speaking at a gathering of leaders in a mainline denomination a number of years ago. When I got to the end of my paper there was a question-and-answer period, and I remember a man standing up who is a professor in one of the theological seminaries. He disagreed with everything I had said, and he took a long time to do it. At one point, because I had mentioned the historical Jesus, he said, "There is no such thing as the historical Jesus. Don't you know that every one of the gospels was written to contradict the other gospels?" (I didn't know that! I thought they were different portraits of the same Christ, that they were complementary.)

Again, at one point in my remarks, I had said that Jesus was going to come again. This professor said, "We have got to get it into our heads that Jesus is never coming back and all things are going to continue as they have from the beginning." Now, that did not surprise me because Peter said precisely this in one of his letters: "In the last days scoffers will come. . . . They will say, 'Where is this coming He promised? For since our fathers died, everything goes on as it has since the beginning of creation' " (2 Peter 3:3–4). That man was quoting it verbatim, though I do not think he knew what he was doing! It was probably the residue of his evangelical upbringing, which he had rebelled against.

But here he was, teaching unbelief to the new ministers in our seminaries.

I have another friend who has worked for renewal in that same denomination. On one occasion, after he had been arguing a point, a liberal minister came up to him and said, "Why are you always quoting the Bible when you stand up to argue a point? Don't you know that nobody believes the Bible anymore?"

Some years ago a news report crossed my desk regarding a three-day national seminar of the Southern Baptist Christian Life Commission. One of the speakers was Robert Bratcher, a main translator of the *Good News for Modern Man* Bible. He said:

> Only willful ignorance or intellectual dishonesty can account for the claim that the Bible is inerrant and infallible . . . . No truth-loving, God-respecting, Christ-honoring believer should be guilty of such heresy. To invest the Bible with the qualities of inerrancy and infallibility is to idolatrize it, to transform it into a false God . . . . Often in the past and still too often in the present to affirm that the Bible is the Word of God implies that the words of the Bible are the words of God. [Yes, I thought that is what we were affirming—always in the past and not nearly enough in the present.] Such simplistic and absolute terms divest the

Bible altogether of its humanity and remove it
from the relativism of the historical process.
No one seriously claims that all the words of
the Bible are the very words of God. [That, at
least, is wrong, because I seriously claim it.]
. . . Quoting what the Bible says in the context
of its history and culture is not necessarily
relevant or helpful, and may be a hindrance in
trying to meet and solve the problems we face.
. . . Even words spoken by Jesus in Aramaic in
the thirties of the first century and preserved
in writing in Greek 35 to 50 years later, do not
necessarily wield compelling or authoritative
authority over us . . . It is the height of presumption and arrogance to say, "I know this is
God's will, and I am doing it."

That is what we are up against, and it is a sad
state of affairs. It is not unnecessary to say that the
men who stand in the pulpit must be born again
and must believe the Bible.

Not only must we who preach believe the Bible,
we must also obey the Bible. Those of us who make
a point of affirming the Bible's authority must take
note of this especially, because it is very easy to
make a crusade of something while not actually allowing it to influence your life. You can wave a
banner. You can say, "Oh, yes, I believe in the
Bible." You can get people to cheer. But then you
can go out and do something that you know is per-

fectly contrary to what the Bible says. You can even know the Bible well enough to quote it back to God and yet disobey it.

Jonah was a preacher who was told to go to Nineveh, and he would not do it. He ran away. Indeed, he was going to Tarshish until God intercepted him and brought him back. God took His election of Jonah to that particular ministry so seriously that in God's sight Jonah was absolutely indispensable. So He brought him back and used him to effect the greatest revival the world has ever seen. At the end of the story Jonah is unhappy, and he explains why it was that he did not obey when God sent him to Nineveh.

Why was it? Was it the danger? Well, Nineveh was a dangerous place. The Ninevites were not nice people. When there was somebody they did not like, they cut off his head. If they had a lot of people they did not like, they cut off all their heads and piled them up in a great pyramid in the city square. It was their idea of a visual aid to learning. Jonah might have said, "I don't want my head on that pile. It's too dangerous. I won't go." Yet there is not a word in the Bible to indicate that this is why he refused.

Was it the difficulty? He might have said, "Me? Jonah? One man? A Jew? How can I possibly influence all those mighty people? I can't do it; I'm just a nobody. I have to stay home." There is not a word to indicate that this was the reason either.

What was it? At the end of the book Jonah says, in effect, "The reason I'm unhappy is that You, O God, caused a revival among the enemies of my people and so spared them. The reason why I wouldn't go to Nineveh in the first place is that I knew that was what You were going to do. You were sending me to preach a message of judgment, to say, 'If you don't repent in forty days, you're going to go to hell.' But you didn't need me to go and tell them they were going to go to hell; they'd have gone to hell without my preaching, and done it just as quickly. You were sending me with a message of judgment so they would repent. And do you want to know how I knew that? I read it in your book. I read it right there in the thirty-second chapter of Exodus, where it says, 'The LORD, the LORD, the compassionate and gracious God, slow to anger, abounding in love and faithfulness, maintaining love to thousands, and forgiving wickedness, rebellion, and sin. Yet He does not leave the guilty unpunished; He punishes the children and their children for the sin of the fathers to the third and fourth generation' " (Exodus 34:6–7; cf. Jonah 4:2). Do you see the problem? It was not a question of Jonah's not knowing the Word or not believing the Word. It was a question of obedience.

God's Enoch

We need preachers who will walk with God. That is, we need preachers who will walk with God in a regular, steady, at times unspectacular and often difficult way, week by week, month by month, year by year, because our work is not always a spectacular business.

A great illustration of this is the walk of the first explicit preacher in the Bible. I told you Luther's opinion of the antedeluvians. He talked about all of them being preachers in their time, and certainly priests in their own home. But most of them are not explicitly said to be preachers. One man is: Enoch. He is mentioned in the fifth chapter of Genesis, where we are told two times over that he "walked with God," and that is why I refer to him.

It is an interesting feature of this man that more is told us about him in the New Testament than is told about him in the Old. There are four verses in the Old Testament as opposed to three in the New, but there are more words in the New than in the Old (ninety words in the New Testament to about fifty in the Old). Jude contains some teaching about him (vv. 14–15), and his name is mentioned in Hebrews 11:5.

Jude identifies Enoch as the "seventh from Adam." Can you think of anybody else in the Bible who is identified as the seventh from anybody, or the fifth, or the third? I cannot, except in the genealogy of Christ where you have fourteen generations from segment to segment. Why is it that Jude refers to Enoch as the seventh from Adam? The reason emerges when you examine that fifth chapter of Genesis in light of the fourth, because in Genesis 4 and 5 you find not one but two Enochs. Genesis 4 gives the line of Cain, the ungodly line. Genesis 5 gives the line of Seth, the godly line. And there is an Enoch in the line of Seth as well as in the line of Cain. Enoch in the line of Cain is the third from Adam, that is, Cain's son. Enoch in the line of Seth is the seventh from Adam. He was the son of Jared, and his son was Methuselah. Jude is saying, "I want to hold up a great example of godly living: Enoch. But I don't want you to make a mistake. I don't want you to imitate the wrong one. God has His Enoch. The devil also has his Enoch. I want you to imitate God's Enoch."

This gives a great principle for understanding much of life. The devil has his people; God has His people. The devil has his doctors; God has His doctors. The devil has his housewives; God has His housewives. The devil has his lawyers; God has His lawyers. Here God is saying, "The devil has his preachers, and I have My preachers. Imitate my men."

Jude also tells us something about Enoch's preaching. He says that he had a message of judgment. As I read Genesis, I think this was new. I think these early believers lived in hope of the coming of the Deliverer, but they did not understand much about His coming. The first messianic prophecy, called the *protoevangelium*, occurs in Genesis 3 in the context of the curse upon the serpent. God said, "I'm sending a deliverer. He'll be the seed of the woman. He'll crush Satan's head, though Satan will bruise His heel" (cf. Genesis 3:15). In those early days this is what Adam and Eve and the others lived in hope of. This is what they looked for. But along came Enoch, who had received this revelation: "God is indeed coming, but before He comes as deliverer He is going to come as judge. There is going to be a flood." His message was, "See, the Lord is coming with thousands upon thousands of His holy ones to judge everyone" (Jude 14–15).

But why is God coming to judge everyone? Because of our wickedness, says Enoch. He is coming "to convict all the ungodly of all the ungodly acts they have done in the ungodly way, and of all the harsh words ungodly sinners have spoken against Him." How many times does Enoch say "ungodly" in that passage? Four times! There are only twenty-eight words in that segment of this passage in my Bible, but four of them are the word "ungodly." One-seventh of all Enoch's recorded preaching focused on the ungodliness of his age.

What is the point? Simply that these concerns go together with what is told about Enoch back in Genesis where it says, "Enoch walked with God." Jude used the word "ungodly" four times, but in Genesis it says twice, "Enoch walked with God." When Enoch had lived 65 years he became the father of Methuselah. And after he became the father of Methuselah, Enoch walked with God 300 years and had other sons and daughters. Altogether Enoch lived 365 years. Enoch walked with God. Enoch began to walk with God in a special way when he was sixty-five years old. I think that is when he got his revelation of coming judgment. He knew what was coming. He saw the ungodliness of his age, and he was now determined. He had believed in God before, but now he was determined to walk with God in the midst of this ungodliness. He walked with God and he walked with God and he walked with God, and when he died at age 365, it says of him, "Enoch walked with God."

That was no casual stroll. Three hundred years is a long time. What kept Enoch walking with God for 300 years? I think these things went together. You have an awareness of judgment coming. You have sensitivity to the ungodliness of the age. And you have the reaction of Enoch, who drew closer to God as the reality of these things pressed in upon him. The way to graph it would be to make a circle, space these three items around the circle and then show by arrows that each one influenced the other. The more Enoch was aware of the judgment, the more sensitive he was to sin. The more sensitive he was to sin, the closer he wanted to walk with God. The closer he walked with God, the more necessary he saw that judgment was. Or the other way: the more he saw the judgment coming, the closer he wanted to walk with God, and the closer he walked with God the more sensitive he was to ungodliness.

If you keep close to God, you will keep from sin. But if you sin you will fall away from God. What will happen then is that you will rename the sin. You will not talk about pride, the great sin; you will call it "self-esteem," or "self-worth," what is "due to me." You will not talk about gluttony and materialism; you will talk about "the good life." You will not talk about disobedience; you will talk about "shortcomings." You will not talk about the Ten Commandments and your violation of them; you will talk about your "mistakes." It is only when you draw close to God that these things will become increasingly sinful in your sight. Then only will they work together to make you a preacher committed to calling men and women to repentance and faith in Christ before the judgment comes.

I mentioned three texts in the Bible that speak about Enoch: Genesis 5:21–24; Jude 14–15 and Hebrews 11:5. I close with this last text because of something that is said there about Enoch: "By faith Enoch was taken from this life, so that he did not experience death; he could not be found, because God had taken him away. For before he was taken, he was commended as one who pleased God."

We are all anxious to please. One reason why we have such a dearth of leadership in our age is that those who could and should be leaders are so anxious to please people, their constituency or their superiors, that they are afraid to lead and so become paralyzed. We all have a desire to please people. We are pleased when people are pleased. When I preach a sermon that I am pleased with and I go to the door and somebody says, "Oh, I really did enjoy that sermon," I am pleased. But, you know, if it comes right down to a choice between pleasing men and pleasing God, there is no choice for the one who claims to be a servant of the Most High. We must please God!

We must so live, so act, so preach and so testify that at the day of final reckoning, when we stand before the One who made us and called us into service, it will not be said of us, "Here is one who sought all through life to please others," but rather, "Here is one who above all else determined to please God." When you seek a minister for your congregation, look for that. Look for someone who is determined to please God. You will be blessed. They will be blessed. And the day will come when the Lord Himself will say to you and to them, "Welcome into My presence, you good and faithful servant. Enter into the joy of your Lord."

Expository Preaching
Keeping Your Eye on the Text

Derek Thomas

According to the legendary golfer, Jack Nicklaus, the best thing he ever did was to discover the "fundamentalist" teacher, Jack Grout, who taught him the basics that he has followed ever since. Great preachers, like great golfers, follow basic rules. The more they practice these rules, the better they become.

One such rule, put succinctly in an English prose that now sounds dated, but is as needful now as when it was first penned, comes from *The Directory for the Publick Worship of God*, written in 1645. When raising a point from the text, preachers are to ensure that "it be a truth contained in or grounded on that text," and "that the hearers may discern how God teacheth it from thence."[1] Preaching must enable those who hear it to understand their Bibles. Thus, whenever the English Reformation produced its first book on homiletics, William Perkins's *The Arte of Prophecying*, in 1617, the book included the instruction,

---

[1] *The Confession of Faith* (The Publications Committee of the Free Presbyterian Church of Scotland, 1970), 379.

> The Word of God alone is to be preached, in its
> perfection and inner consistency. Scripture is
> the exclusive subject of preaching, the only
> field in which the preacher is to labour.[2]

It may sound elementary, but Perkins found it
necessary to underline that preachers preach the
Bible and the Bible *alone*. "Preach the word," Paul
urged Timothy (2 Timothy 4:2), having earlier assured the Corinthians that he was not "like so
many, peddlers of God's Word" (2 Corinthians
2:17). The word Paul employs, *kapeleuô*, is rendered
variously as "peddle," "corrupt," or "deal deceit-
fully," or as the New Living Translation renders it,
"we are not like those hucksters—and there are
many of them—who preach just to make money."
This word comes from the world of ancient tavern-
keeping. It suggests the practice of "blending, adul-
terating, and giving bad measure."[3] Paul is concerned for purity and honesty in handling the
Scriptures. He charges young Timothy again to
present himself to God "as one approved, a worker
who has no need to be ashamed, rightly handling

---

[2] William Perkins, *The Art of Prophesying* (Edinburgh: The
Banner of Truth, 1996), 9.

[3] James Denney, *The Expositor's Bible*, New Edition, *The
Second Epistle to the Corinthians* (London: Hodder &
Stoughton, 1916), 97. Tyndale rendered the verse, "We are
not of those who chop and change the Word of God."

the word of truth" (2 Timothy 2:15). The word, translated in many versions as either "to handle" or "to divide" is actually a word that means to cut (*orthotomeo*).[4] Timothy is to ensure that he drives a straight path through the Word of God and not deviate to the left or to the right. He is to "preach the word," meaning not only that he is to preach from the Bible, but that he is to *expound* the particular passage he is preaching on because Scripture, as Paul has just reminded Timothy, is "God-breathed" (2 Timothy 3:16).

Expository preaching is a *necessary* corollary of the doctrine of the God-breathed nature of Scripture. The idea is not so much that God breathed *into* the Scriptures, but that the Scriptures are the product of His breathing *out*. Independent of what we may feel regarding the Bible as we read it, Scripture maintains a "breath of God" quality. The preacher is to make God's word known and make it understandable. He is to limit himself to it without adding or subtracting. As Alec Motyer has written,

---

[4] A New Testament *hapax legomenon*, Arndt and Gingrich render *orthotomeo* "to "guide the word of truth along a straight path." W. F. Arndt and F. W. Gingrich, *A Greek-English Lexicon of the New Testament and Other Early Christian Literature*, 4th ed. (Chicago, Ill.: The University of Chicago Press, [1957] 1974), 584.

> An expository ministry is the proper re-
> sponse to a God-breathed Scripture. . . .
> Central to it all is that concern which the word
> 'exposition' itself enshrines: a display of what
> is there.[5]

Such word-focused ministry, based on divinely given Scripture (as Paul makes plain to the church at Ephesus), fulfills four goals all at once: it builds up the church in faith and knowledge; it brings believers to maturity marked by spiritual stability; it produces a people whose lives are full of integrity; and it equips the church for service so that each member is engaged in ministry to others (Ephesians 4:12–16).

From Calvin to Boice

Belief in the divine origin of Scripture led John Calvin in the sixteenth century to a commitment to expository/exegetical preaching. Commenting on 2 Timothy 3:16–17, the *locus classicus* of biblical inspiration, the Genevan Reformer insisted that,

> We owe to the Scriptures the same reverence
> as we owe to God, since it has its only source

---

[5] Foreword to the British edition of Haddon Robinson's *Expository Preaching: Principles and Practice* (Leicester: Inter-Varsity Press, 1980), vi.

in Him and has nothing of human origin mixed with it.[6]

Therefore, the preaching of Scripture requires the most thorough preparation. At the same time that Calvin preached through 1 and 2 Timothy on Sundays, he was preaching on Job and then Deuteronomy on weekdays. Commenting on Deuteronomy 6:16, Calvin has this to say:

> If I should step up into the pulpit, without vouchsafing to look upon any book, and fondly imagine to say thus in my self, 'Truth, when I come thither, God will give me enough whereof to speak,' and in the mean while I hold scorn to read, or to study aforehand what I shall speak, and come hither without minding how to apply the Holy Scripture to the edification of the people, by reason whereof I should play the presumptuous fool, and God would put me to shame for mine overboldness.[7]

---

[6] John Calvin, *Calvin's New Testament Commentaries: The Second Epistle of Paul to the Corinthians, and the Epistles to Timothy, Titus and Philemon,* trans. T. A. Small, eds. David W. Torrance and Thomas F. Torrance (Grand Rapids, Mich.: Eerdmans, 1991), 330.

[7] John Calvin, *Sermons on Deuteronomy,* Facsimile edition of 1583 (Edinburgh: The Banner of Truth Trust, 1987), 292, Column 1. The sermon is the 49th on Deuteronomy. The

Though Calvin is fond of the word "dictation" when he refers to the inspiration of Scripture,[8] it does not mean that Calvin saw no place for, or implications derived from, the *humanness* of Scripture. Early in the *Institutes* he comments on the "elegant" and "brilliant" style of some of the prophets, the "sweet" and "pleasing" styles of David and Isaiah, or the "harsher" styles of Amos, Jeremiah, and Zechariah.[9] Thus Calvin gave due diligence to the meaning of the words of Scripture, to grammar and syntax, to literary genre, to authorial intent, to context, and to a hermeneutic of harmony that a belief in inspiration requires. But at the end of the day, Calvin could say in his last will and testament,

> I have endeavored, both in my sermons and also in my writings and commentaries, to preach the Word purely and chastely, and

---

Elizabethan spelling has been updated for our purposes here. Cf. T. H. L. Parker, *Calvin's Preaching* (Louisville, Ky.: Westminster/John Knox Press, 1992), 81.

[8] See *The Institutes of the Christian Religion*, 2 vols., trans. Ford Lewis Battles, ed. John T. McNeill (Philadelphia, Pa.: The Westminster Press, 1975), 2:1154 [IV.viii.6]. For other examples, see David L. Puckett, John Calvin's *Exegesis of the Old Testament* (Louisville, Ky.: The Westminster Press/John Knox, 1995), 26-27.

[9] *The Institutes of the Christian Religion*, 1:83 [I.viii.2].

faithfully to interpret His sacred Scriptures.[10]

During the years 1549–1560, Calvin employed Denis Ragunier to record word for word every sermon he preached. Over two thousand of his sermons exist today for us to examine and from which to profit, and what continues to amaze is their consistency of style. Though Calvin never wrote a formal manual on homiletics, his sermons disclose a commitment to the discipline of expository preaching and the *lectio continua* method. As for the latter, it is not essential to do what Calvin did (or the "golden-mouthed" Chrysostom before him[11]), that is, to preach consecutively through the books of the Bible (in Calvin's case) 6–10 verses at a time. Textual sermons can and should be equally expository, that is, committed to the discipline of sound exegetical principles. But history reveals that the benefits of the *lectio continua* method of preaching are considerable and essential in eras of biblical illiteracy. Nothing could illustrate Calvin's commitment to it better than the fact that following

---

[10] Theodore Beza, *The Life of John Calvin*, ed. Gary Sanseri [reprint of Calvin Translation Society, 1844, ed. and trans. Henry Beveridge] (Milwaukee, Oreg.: Back Home Industries, 1996), 100.

[11] Chrysostom was known in the sixth century by the term *chrysostomos*, or "golden-mouthed."

his enforced exile in Strasbourg (having been evicted from Geneva on Easter Day 1538), Calvin returned in September of 1541 to pick up precisely where he had left off three and half years before.[12]

In our own time, few have raised the importance of expository preaching within the discipline of homiletics more than the quartet: Bryan Chapell, John MacArthur, Martyn Lloyd-Jones and James Montgomery Boice. Each one has contributed to the conviction of the value *and necessity* of expository preaching. Chapell's 1994 "Book of the Year," *Christ-centered Preaching*, bearing the subtitle, "*Redeeming the Expository Sermon*," is justly applauded quite simply as one of the best one-volumed works on preaching to emerge in a century.[13] In it he defines an expository sermon as that which

> requires that it expound Scripture by deriving from a specific text main points and subpoints that disclose the thought of the author, cover the scope of the passage, and are applied to the lives of the listeners.[14]

---

[12] T. H. L. Parker, *Calvin's Preaching*, 60.

[13] Bryan Chapell, *Christ-Centered Preaching* (Grand Rapids, Mich.: Baker Books, 1994). In 1992, Chapell produced the now-revised work on sermon illustrations, *Using Illustrations to Preach with Power* (Wheaton, Ill.: Crossway, [1992], 2001).

[14] *Christ-Centered Preaching,* 129. Haddon Robinson's equally well-known definition still has force: "Expository preaching is

Chapell has done more than most to recover a zeal for expository preaching amongst his own constituents and beyond. Not that he is without detractors. Some have commented that much expository preaching is so bad that it calls into question the method. That bad expository preaching exists cannot be denied. Much of it is in the form of a running commentary, with little attention to struc-

---

the communication of a biblical concept, derived from and transmitted through a historical, grammatical, and literary study of a passage in its context, which the Holy Spirit first applies to the personality and experience of the preacher, then through the preacher, applies to the hearers." *Biblical Preaching: The Development and Delivery of Expository Messages* 2nd ed. (Grand Rapids, Mich.: Baker Books, [1980] 2001), 21. In the nineteenth century, William Taylor defined it in simpler form this way: "By expository preaching, I mean that method of pulpit discourse which consists in the consecutive interpretation, and practical enforcement, of a book of sacred canon." *The Ministry of the Word* (Grand Rapids, Mich.: Baker Books, 1975), 155. My own favorite definition comes from Alan M. Stibbs's little book, *Expounding God's Word* (London: Inter-Varsity Press [1960] 1970), when he writes: "The business of the preacher is to stick to the passage chosen and to set forth exclusively what it has to say or suggest, so that the ideas expressed and the principles enunciated during the course of the sermon plainly come out of the Written Word of God, and have its authority for their support rather than just the opinion or the enthusiasm of their human expositor" (17).

ture and form. As one who now teaches homiletics at a seminary, I find myself needing to distinguish a sermon from something that sounds like the fruits of culling several commentaries (even if they are *good* ones!). The necessary discipline of understanding the text is only the first step in constructing a sermon. There is more to preaching than imparting information, and Chapell is insistent on it. Unless sermons address the affections, they have failed as sermons. In the deceptively simple advice of the Cambridge preacher, Charles Simeon (1759-1836),

> The understanding must be informed, but in a manner, however, which *affects the heart*, either to comfort the hearers, or to excite them to acts of piety, repentance, or holiness.[15]

John MacArthur writes in *Rediscovering Expository Preaching*, "The only logical response to inerrant Scripture, then, is to preach it *expositionally*."[16] Defining *exegesis* as "the skillful application

---

[15] The words come from his "Hints on Writing Sermons" in *Let Wisdom Judge,* ed. Arthur Pollard (London: Inter-Varsity Press, 1959), 22. This, he adds, is best done by way of "perpetual application."

[16] John MacArthur, Jr. and the Master's Seminary Faculty, *Rediscovering Expository Preaching*, ed. Richard L. Mayhue and Robert L. Thomas (Dallas, Tx.: Word, 1992), 23.

of sound hermeneutical principles to the biblical text of the original language with a view to understanding and declaring the author's intended meaning both to the immediate and subsequent audiences."[17] MacArthur insists that the church's loss of commitment to expository preaching is due to what he calls "the legacy of liberalism." Robbed of any confidence in the Scriptures themselves through textual or source criticism, preachers lost sight of the goal: making the Scriptures known. Instead of explaining the Scriptures, preachers felt the need to apologize for much of its content and supply their own rhetorical skills to make up for the deficiency. MacArthur is right: only in the context of a firm belief in Scripture's inerrancy has expository preaching thrived.

Dr. Martyn Lloyd-Jones's lectures at Westminster Seminary (Philadelphia) in the Spring of 1969 resulted in what has proved to be a classic work on preaching in the twentieth century, *Preachers and Preaching*.[18] It is hard to imagine not having read and profited from this book. It covers a wide variety of issues and in one sense is much more than a work on the *mechanics* of preaching. It contains the reflections of a great preacher eager to inculcate

---

[17] *Ibid.* 29.
[18] D. Martyn Lloyd-Jones, *Preaching and Preachers* (Grand Rapids, Mich.: Zondervan, 1971).

much more than *how* to construct a sermon. Early
in the book, Lloyd-Jones issues a warning about
abusing Scripture by making it fit a particular system of truth. It betrays his concern for proper exe-
cution of exegetical disciplines in preaching:

> It is wrong for a man to impose his system
> violently on any particular text; but at the
> same time it is vital that his interpretation of
> any particular text should be checked and con-
> trolled by this system, this body of doctrine
> and of truth which is found in the Bible. The
> tendency of some men who have a systematic
> theology, which they hold very rigidly, is to
> impose this wrongly upon particular texts and
> so do violence to those texts. In other words
> they do not actually derive that particular doc-
> trine from the text with which they are dealing
> at that point. The doctrine may be true but it
> does not arise from that particular text; and we
> must always be textual. That is what I meant
> by not 'imposing' your system upon a par-
> ticular text or statement. The right use of sys-
> tematic theology is, that when you discover a
> particular doctrine in your text you check it,
> and control it, by making sure that it fits into
> the whole body of biblical doctrine which is vi-
> tal and essential.[19]

---

[19] *Ibid.* 66–67.

James Montgomery Boice believed in expository preaching and said so often. His four-volume set of sermons on Romans is rightly called *An Expositional Commentary*,[20] as is his five-volume set of sermons on John's Gospel,[21] and similar works on Acts,[22] the Minor Prophets,[23] Genesis,[24] the Psalms,[25] Ephesians,[26] and Philippians.[27] These were sermons before they ever saw the printed format in which we now read them. They are classic in style: simple, structured, highlighting main themes, alluding to other passages only to illustrate what is already drawn out of the text in question, and always applicatory. Few pulpits in the twentieth

---

[20] *Romans: An Expositional Commentary*, 4 vols. (Grand Rapids, Mich.: Baker Books, 1995).
[21] *The Gospel of John: An Expositional Commentary* (Grand Rapids, Mich.: Zondervan Publishing House, 1985).
[22] *Acts: An Expository Commentary* (Grand Rapids, Mich.: Baker Books, 1997).
[23] *The Minor Prophets: An Expositional Commentary*, 2 vols. (Grand Rapids, Mich.: Zondervan, 1983).
[24] *Genesis: An Expositional Commentary*, 3 vols. (Grand Rapids, Mich.: Baker Books, 1988)
[25] *The Psalms: An Expositional Commentary*, 3 vols. (Grand Rapids, Mich.: Baker Books, 1994)
[26] *Ephesians: An Expositional Commentary* (Grand Rapids, Mich.: Baker Books, 1997).
[27] *Philippians: An Expositional Commentary* (Grand Rapids, Mich.: Baker Books, 2000).

century enjoyed such rich fare as did Tenth
Presbyterian Church in Philadelphia during his
tenure.

Bad Homiletical Models

Despite these books on preaching, bad homiletical models of expository preaching exist. They
come from various sources and are influenced by a
variety of factors. Often it is not the model itself
that is at fault, but the use made of it. They include:

1. *The Puritans.* Can I possibly say this in a book
published by a company wholly devoted to making
the Puritans known again? Yes, I think I can. But I
feel the need to underline my own commitment to
the Puritans. Few men have influenced my thinking
more than John Owen, unless it is John Calvin. I
owe to the former an understanding of
sanctification and biblical spirituality that has kept
my sanity on more than one occasion. Owen's
works are deservedly reprinted and studied. If ban-
ished to a desert island, with the Bible and 6
books, I would bend every rule to ensure that all
sixteen volumes were included as *one* book, and if
not, then I would have to ensure that Volume 2, *On
Communion with God*, was one of the six![28] To a

---

[28] John Owen, *The Works of John Owen*, ed. William H. Gould.
16 vols. (London: The Banner of Truth, 1972). There is also

man, the Puritans were committed to the *plain*
preaching of the Word of God. Few have matched
the expositional skills of Joseph Hall, Thomas
Goodwin, John Owen, Richard Sibbes, Richard
Baxter, Thomas Manton, Stephen Charnock, or
John Bunyan. On exegetical grounds they stand
shoulder to shoulder with the Denneys and
Lightfoots and Murrays of later centuries. The
church would be greatly impoverished without
Manton on James, Greenhill on Ezekiel, or Jenkyn
on Jude. Their insights and contribution continue
to profit the church. Nevertheless, in the matter of
consecutive expository preaching, the Puritans are
not always a model for us to follow. When Joseph
Caryl (to take an extreme example, to be sure) took
24 years to expound the Book of Job in 424 sermons (averaging ten sermons per chapter), we can
safely say that this does not provide a good model
for preaching the Book of Job or for expository
preaching generally.[29] They show an admirable

---

the recent translation from the Latin of his *Biblical Theology*
(Morgan, Pa.: Soli Deo Gloria, 1994), and the seven-volume
commentary on Hebrews, *An Exposition of the Epistle to the
Hebrews* (Grand Rapids, Mich.: Baker Books, 1980).

[29] The sermons have recently been reprinted in 12 volumes
jointly by Dust and Ashes Publications and Reformed
Heritage Books (2001) and contain an endorsement as to
their perennial value by me!

care in teasing out doctrine and even greater skill in application to those in diverse trials (it is this that makes them invaluable reading still), but it is doubtful if there are any circumstances, then or now, that would justify such a prolonged series of sermons on one book. Speaking generally is always dangerous, but it is probably true to say that few young preachers can sustain lengthy (and slow) series of expositions on a particular book of the Bible. Times have changed, as have our congregations, and it is wiser in most circumstances to move at a more rapid pace through the Scriptures than the Puritans were wont to do.

2. *Dr. Martyn Lloyd-Jones.* Possibly the greatest expositor/preacher of the twentieth century, Lloyd-Jones has had a considerable influence on the preaching styles of several generations of preachers on both sides of the Atlantic. In Britain especially, following the publication of Martyn Lloyd-Jones's expositions of Romans (sermons preached during the thirteen year period, 1955-1968), many Reformed preachers attempted to do the same.[30] The problem was that few, if any, could come close to the exegetical and homiletical skills of "the Doctor." Many a congregation was wearied by an

---

[30] The first volume, on Romans 3:20-4:25 appeared in 1970 and since then another eleven volumes have appeared. They are published by The Banner of Truth Trust.

overly ambitious series in the consecutive expository method, and by practitioners that weren't up to the task. What may have been possible and desirable in that context, may not be in our own—and that due to several factors, including the giftedness and maturity of the preacher together with the makeup of the congregation.[31] Some preachers have been drained by an overly-ambitious series that was beyond their giftedness to deliver. In consequence, they have retreated to safer shores.

3. *C. H. Spurgeon.* The Anglican Bishop J. C. Ryle, in a wonderful lecture called "Simplicity in Preaching" given at St. Paul's Cathedral, said of Spurgeon's preaching,

> I am not a bit ashamed to say that I often read the sermons of Mr. Spurgeon. I like to gather hints about preaching from all quarters.... Now when you read Mr. Spurgeon's sermons, note how clearly and perspicuously he divides a sermon, and fills each division with beautiful

---

[31] The "sermons" were delivered on a Friday evening rather than on Sundays, a fact that many imitators failed to observe. The audience, therefore, was very different, comprising ardent and enthusiastic admirers of "the Doctor's" preaching style. Some traveled long distances every week in order to be there. Though they comprise some of the finest preaching on Romans ever to have been done, it is doubtful whether most preachers have the gifting to mimic it.

> and simple ideas. How easily you grasp the
> meaning! . . . great truths, that hang to you
> like hooks of steel, and which . . . you never
> forget![32]

My own acquaintance with, and love for,
Spurgeon came in 1977 when a somewhat disillu-
sioned friend offered me the complete set (62 volumes) of his sermons, which he had just purchased and had found wanting! I have used them
over and over ever since, sometimes with great de-
light and admiration, and sometimes (it has to be
said) with dismay at his handling of the text.[33]
Spurgeon's invariable style was textual, often focus-
ing on one or two verses.[34] His intent was always to
be expository; in practice, he could sometimes
introduce matters into the sermon that did not
properly emerge from the text, and he never engaged in consecutive expository preaching. The in-

---

[32] J. C. Ryle, *The Upper Room* (London: The Banner of Truth
Trust, [1888], 1970), 42. Cf. J. I. Packer, *Faithfulness and
Holiness: The Witness of J. C. Ryle* (Wheaton, Ill.: Crossway,
2002), 62.

[33] The complete set was published by Pilgrim Publications
(Pasadena, Tex.) in 1977.

[34] Only Spurgeon could preach on the text, "Until he find it"
in Luke 15:4, for example! The sermon was preached on
Thursday evening, June 28, 1877, and can be found in volume 49.

fluence of the greatest Baptist preacher of the nineteenth century has been too considerable to calculate.

4. *Redemptive-historical preaching.* There is a view of redemptive-historical preaching currently that is deeply critical of expository preaching styles of the past. It is a view that regards the homiletical styles of Augustine and Calvin as guilty of mixing Judeo-Christian theology with classical pagan methodology in its use of the grammatico-historical hermeneutic. It is not altogether clear what the overall agenda of this school of thought is, but it is severely critical of past and present attempts at exegetical preaching. There is still a commitment to preaching the text and even doing so consecutively; as such, it has all the feel of expository preaching. But there is a concern (a valid concern it must be said) to emphasize context within the overall structure of God's redemptive plan as it unfolds historically. Sermons of this sort spend a great deal of time detailing the flow of redemptive history which, on first hearing, can be breathtaking if done well. But what often results from this hermeneutic has a sameness to it (a rehearsal of the history of redemption) that those who have heard it repeatedly regard as "boring" and "irrelevant." Indeed, in its fear of moralistic exegesis (*biographical* preaching is particularly criticized), application is noticeably

absent from these sermons. There is much appeal
to the mind, but little if any to the heart. Indeed,
many sermons in this school of thought have no
discernible application whatsoever, apart from the
informative, that shapes the way we think. Some of
the remarks in an otherwise masterly treatment of
preaching by Sidney Greidanus, falls under this
criticism.[35]

These, and other considerations, have led some
in a direction away from consecutive expository
preaching. Some have found refuge in textual
preaching. Such preaching, as we said, can often
be decidedly exegetical in nature. The sermon
sticks to the text and seeks to expound the passage
(or verse) according to the rules of sound interpretation. It is a method that has much to commend
it, not least in that each Lord's Day brings forth
"something new" that frees the preacher from the
charge of predictability and sameness.

When the Eye Is Not on the Text

There are a variety of sermon types that fail to
"display what is there." These include:

1. The *"I want to tell you what is on my heart"* ser-

---

[35] Sidney Greidanus, *The Modern Preacher and the Ancient Text*
(Grand Rapids, Mich.: Eerdmans; Leicester: Inter-Varsity
Press, 1996).

mon. It may begin with the text, but the text functions as a mere peg on which to hang the preacher's "concerns." Its hermeneutic is inadequate. It fails to look at the intention of God in the passage. What emerges is often full of passion but devoid of precision, earnest but effervescent, relevant but *un*-related.

2. The "*I have been reading* Berkhof's *Systematic Theology*" sermon.[36] Instead of asking the question, "What is the intention of God?" it asks, "Where does this passage fit in my systematic theology?" or, "What doctrine does this passage teach?" Both Reformed and Dispensational schools fall into this regularly. They have a certain shape of truth, and this shape is going to be stretched and made to fit. Sermons become defensive. These sermons are often better when dealing with Pauline epistles but go hopelessly astray when dealing in the genres of poetry or history. The sermons are often careful, too careful in avoiding the barriers established by systematic theology, but fail to come right up close to them as many texts of Scripture will force us to

---

[36] This is *not* a criticism of systematic theology. After all, I am gainfully employed teaching systematic theology to seminary students and happen to think that Berkhof is essential reading! Louis Berkhof, *Systematic Theology* (Edinburgh: The Banner of Truth, [1939], 1971).

do. In order to make the passage fit, it must be bent out of shape, and the result looks very different from what a cursory reading of the passage will suggest.[37]

3. The *"I have a seminary education and I am determined to let you know that"* sermon. In its extreme form it becomes a lecture on the original meaning of the Greek or Hebrew. What belongs in the preacher's study is brought into the pulpit. There is enormous emphasis on the word study, syntax, Greek and/or Hebrew, archeology, textual variants, original intent, and cultural background. The research is vast and has had as its aim a proper exegesis of the passage. But it has failed to "bridge the gap between two horizons" (to borrow the language of Gadamer and Thiselton, and popularized by John Stott)[38] stretching from the world of the Bible

---

[37] See Donald Macleod, "Preaching and Systematic Theology," in *The Preacher and Preaching: Reviving the Art in the Twentieth* Century (Philipsburg, N.J.: Presbyterian and Reformed Publishing Company, 1986), 246-274; J. I. Packer, "The Preacher as Theologian" in *When God's Voice Is Heard: Essays on Preaching Presented to Dick Lucas*, ed. Christopher Green and David Jackman (Leicester: Inter-Varsity Press, 1995), 79-96. Also Sinclair B. Ferguson's essay, "The Preacher as Theologian" in *The Practical Preacher: Practical Wisdom for the Pastor-Preacher* (Fern, Rosshire: Christian Focus Publications, 2002), 103–115.

[38] See John R. W. Stott *Between Two Worlds: The Challenge of*

to the world of the listener. It sounds like, and is, a lecture. It has titillated the intellect, but failed entirely to minister to the affections. Its research has even created a Gnostic view that only the few—those endowed by a special wisdom and insight—can possibly be trusted to understand what the Bible says. The sermon fails to underline the Reformational emphasis on the perspicuity of Scripture: "that not only the learned, but the unlearned, in a due use of the ordinary means, may attain a sufficient understanding of them."[39] A Reformed sacerdotalism has emerged, with the preacher squarely resident between the Bible and the listener.

4. The "*I am in such a hurry to apply this that you must forgive me for not showing you where I get this from*" sermon. The necessary study may well have been done, but the listener is unable to "discern how God teacheth it from thence." Listeners gain the impression that they are being lectured at, that some hidden (and maybe not so hidden) agenda is at work. They do not come away having understood the passage better or with the impression that they could have discerned this for themselves.

Preaching Today (Grand Rapids, Mich.: Eerdmans, [1982] 1994).
39 Westminster Confession of Faith, I.7.

The *Lectio Continua* Method

While it is, of course, possible (and sometimes desirable) to preach expository sermons *textually*—in Romans this week, in the Psalms the next, and in Haggai the following week—there is something about the very discipline of exposition that makes it impossible not to pick up the threads of an argument that begins in a previous chapter and runs on for several more. Few are the passages that are complete in themselves, that require little, if any, reference to preceding verses or what follows (the Psalms taken as *whole psalms* is one example, though not if only one or two verses of a psalm constitute the text). It is very difficult to read Paul without following a lengthy argument that unfolds over lengthy passages requiring a *series* of sermons to unpack. It might be helpful, then, to ask, "What are some of the advantages and disadvantages of the *consecutive* expository sermon?"[40] These can be summarized this way:

1. According to Archibald Alexander, one benefit of expository preaching is that it introduces the congregation to the entire Bible.

---

[40] Though dated, John A. Broadus's justly famous work on homiletics is still of enormous value. *A Treatise on the Preparation and Delivery of Sermons,* 2nd ed. (London: James Nisbet & Co., 1871). He has some useful things to say about expository preaching on pages 299-318.

> ...all the more cardinal books of Scripture should be fully expounded in every church, if not once during the life of a single preacher, certainly during each generation; in order that no man should grow up without opportunity of hearing the great body of scriptural truth laid open.[41]

In an age of relative illiteracy as far as the contents of Scripture is concerned in many parts of the world, the need to preach the whole Bible, rather than serendipitously picking a text from here and there, is all the more urgent. Writing over a century ago, William Taylor opined,

> I have seen a slimly attended second service gather back into itself all the half-day hearers that had absented themselves from it, and draw in others besides, through the adoption by the minister of just such a method as this; while the effect, even upon those who have dropped casually in upon a single discourse, has been to send them away with what one of themselves called "a new appetite for the Word of God.[42]

---

[41] J. W. Alexander, *Thoughts on Preaching* (Edinburgh: The Banner of Truth Trust, [1864] 1975), 237.
[42] *The Ministry of the Word,* 161.

2. It ensures that infrequently traveled areas of the Bible are covered. The *theopneustic* quality of Scripture (2 Timothy 3:16–17) implies that the whole canon—"all Scripture" (*pasa graphe*)—bears the mark of divine authorship. Our knowledge and holiness are hampered to the degree we neglect certain portions of Scripture. What preacher will select from Zechariah, or Jeremiah, or Revelation (except it be a favorite text or two), unless driven to it by a programmatic attempt to preach through the whole Bible? Large tracts of the Bible will never be touched unless the discipline of consecutive expository preaching forces the preacher to do so.

3. Preachers unwittingly shape the way their hearers read their Bibles. Consecutive expository preaching can inculcate sound habits of personal Bible study. Large areas of the Bible are rarely read by many Christians. They arouse greater dread than the "Mines of Moria" did for Gandalf and Aragorn in *The Fellowship of the Ring*.[43] Consequently, the Bible is reduced to favorite verses, underlined or highlighted to provide stepping stones through murky waters. The necessary principles of sound interpretation can be absorbed, almost by osmosis, through such repeated forays

---

[43] Part 1 of the trilogy *The Lord of the Rings* by J. R. R. Tolkien.

into relatively obscure passages from week to week
in the pulpit. When Paul asked the church at
Colossae to pray that he might be able to preach
"plainly" (Gk. *phanerosis*, unveiling, exposition) he
was asking that he might bring out from the text
what was inherently there. Paul, likewise, made the
claim with respect to his preaching at Corinth, that
"by the open statement of the truth" he refused "to
tamper with God's word" (2 Corinthians 4:2, ESV).
By renouncing distortion (tampering), the apostle
insists that what he did was to "expose" (Gk.
phanerosis) what was already there in the Word.
Hearing that done, week after week, cannot but
cement form and content. It is one of the most
heart-enriching experiences for any preacher to
hear someone bring something out of a text that
reflects (albeit unwittingly) what they have heard
done countless times in the pulpit.[44] As Dabney put
it,

> A prime object of pastoral teaching is to teach
> the people how to read the Bible for them-
> selves. A sealed book cannot be interesting. If
> it be read without the key of comprehension, it
> cannot be instructive. Now, it is the preacher's

---

[44] Cf. Sinclair Ferguson, "Exegesis" in *The Preacher and
Preaching*, ed. Samuel T. Logan, Jr. (Phillipsburg, N.J.:
Presbyterian and Reformed Publishing Company, 1986), 210.

business, in his public discourses, to give his
people teaching by example, in the art of inter-
preting the Word: he should exhibit before
them, in actual use, the methods by which the
legitimate meaning is to be evolved. Fragmentary preaching, however brilliant, will never
do this.[45]

John Stott, in an interview given in 1995, speaks
to this issue:

We want to let the congregation into the secret
as to how we have reached the conclusions we
have reached as to what the Bible is actually
saying. . . . And gradually, as you are doing
this in the pulpit, the congregation is schooled
not only in what the Bible teaches but in how
we come to the congregation as to what it
teaches. So we have to show the congregation
what our hermeneutical methods are.[46]

4. Only by the discipline of consecutive exposi-

---

[45] R. L. Dabney, *Lectures on Sacred Rhetoric* (Edinburgh: The
Banner of Truth Trust, 1870), 81. The book now appears
under the new title, *Evangelical Eloquence: A Course of
Lectures on Preaching* (Edinburgh: The Banner of Truth Trust,
1999).
[46] "Rehabilitating Discipleship: An Interview with John
Stott" in *Prism*, July-August 1995. Cited in *John Stott: A
Biography. The Later Years,* by Timothy Dudley-Smith
(Downers Grove, Ill.: InterVarsity Press, 2001), 335.

tory preaching will a congregation be exposed to the full range of Scripture's interests and concerns.[47] Why would a preacher desire to choose as his subject divorce, or polygamy, or incest other than the fact that they arise naturally in the course of exposition?[48] Many a hearer will accuse preachers of a conspiracy whenever the Word begins to "meddle" (as they say in Mississippi). Happy is the preacher who can just point to the text and say, "It just happens to be the passage we were meant to deal with this morning!" It is only by the sustained use of the *lectio continua* method that large tracts of Scripture can hopefully be covered, including those areas less well known and traversed but containing truth designed to shape us into Christ's image.

5. It is not an unworthy consideration to desire to sustain a congregation's interest from week to week by *variety*. If variety is the spice of life, then

---

[47] Cf. J. W. Alexander, *Thoughts on Preaching*, 234 235.

[48] Again, Dabney is succinct when he suggests that "the expository method enables the pastor to introduce without offence those delicate subjects of temptation and duty, and those obnoxious doctrines and rebukes, which, on the opposite method, always incur so much *odium*. The fragmentary preacher will find it a very difficult and delicate thing to request his charge to give him the Sabbath hour for the discussion of polygamy, of divorce, or of other sins against chastity." *Lectures on Sacred Rhetoric*, 83-84.

the pulpit needs to show it by a preaching style
that reflects something of a great journey, with ever-
changing landscapes and challenges. What makes
Tolkien's epic tale, *The Lord of the Rings*, so utterly
spellbinding is the sheer variety of its style.
Moments of intense drama are interspersed with
slow-moving developments of character and background. The latter is indispensable for the former,
and, indeed, without those less-hurried moments,
the dramatic sections would lose their power.
Suddenly dipping into the journey through the
Mines of Moria to the Bridge at Khazad-dûm would
make no sense unless we had journeyed with them
all the way from Rivendell and, indeed, from
Hobbiton itself. Not every sermon is explosive in
nature, and it is only in the discipline of consecutive expository preaching that the necessary
elements can be set in place for the drama and
excitement of certain passages to have their
intended effect. Bad models of this practice do
exist. It is dangerous to generalize, but preachers
who move too slowly weary their listeners by taking
short texts of one or two verses, or worse, repeating
the same passage for several weeks. To preach
twenty or thirty sermons on the five verses of the
Lord's Prayer in Matthew 6 seems to be an ex-
travagance that only very special circumstances

(not to mention preaching gifts!) can support.[49]

6. Nothing I know better aids preachers in thinking ahead and preparing ahead than this discipline of consecutive expository preaching. Not only does it free preachers from the tyranny of having to choose a text (and then choosing another, and then another when the text fails to yield to the preacher's tapping![50]), it also enables him to be thinking well ahead. Certain themes can receive greater and lesser emphasis knowing that an occasion will come again soon, in the next chapter perhaps, for a more sustained examination of them. Every book of the Bible contains passages which are "hard to understand" (2 Peter 3:16), and preparation for these can take place well in advance.

Faithful expository preaching, whether textual or consecutive, is "a most exacting discipline" according to John Stott. He adds,

Perhaps that is why it is so rare. Only those

---

[49] Dabney is again pertinent: "The expository method is also naturally adapted to sustain the interest of common minds, in that it provides them with frequent and easy transitions of subject. To be held long to the contemplation of the same abstract thought is exceedingly irksome to them" *Ibid.* 87.

[50] I sometimes liken sermon outlining to a certain chocolate product in the shape of an orange that needs to be "tapped" on a hard surface for the segments to fall apart.

will undertake it who are prepared to follow the example of the apostles and say, "It is not right that we should give up preaching the Word of God and serve tables. . . . We will devote ourselves to prayer and to the ministry of the Word" (Acts 6:2, 4). The systematic preaching of the Word is impossible without the systematic study of it. It will not be enough to skim through a few verses in daily Bible reading, nor to study a passage only when we have to preach from it. No. We must daily soak ourselves in the Scriptures. We must not just study, as through a microscope, the linguistic minutiae of a few verses, but take out our telescope and scan the wide expanses of God's Word, assimilating its grand theme of divine sovereignty in the redemption of mankind. "It is blessed," wrote C. H. Spurgeon, "to eat into the very soul of the Bible until, at last, you come to talk in Scriptural language, and your spirit is flavoured with the words of the Lord, so that your blood is Bibline and the very essence of the Bible flows from you."[51]

Commenting upon the preaching of Dr. Martyn Lloyd-Jones, J. I. Packer writes:

---

[51] John R. W. Stott, *The Preacher's Portrait* (Grand Rapids, Mich.: Eerdmans, 1961), 30-31.

I have never known anyone whose speech
communicated such a sense of the reality of
God as did the Doctor in those occasional moments of emphasis and doxology. Most of the
time, however, it was clear, steady analysis,
refection, correction and instruction, based on
simple thoughts culled from the text, set out in
good order with the minimum of extraneous
illustration or decoration. He knew that God's
way to the heart is through the mind (he often
insisted that the first thing the gospel does to a
man is to make him think), and he preached in
a way designed to help people think and
thereby grasp truth—and in the process be
grasped by it, and so be grasped by the God
whose truth it is.[52]

In the end, that is what we desperately need today: preaching that unpacks the Bible's message
and conveys a sense of the reality of God's presence. In the end, only faithful *expository* preaching
can do that.

---

[52] J. I. Packer, "David Martyn Lloyd-Jones" in *Honouring the
People of God,* vol. 4 of *Collected Shorter Writings of J. I.
Packer* (Carlisle, Cumbria: Paternoster, 1999), 85.

The Lasting Power of Reformed Experiential Preaching

Joel R. Beeke

While I was on active duty in the U.S. Army Reserves, a sergeant laid his hand on my shoulder one day and said, "Son, if you ever have to go to war, there are three things you must remember in battle: what tactics you need to use, how the fight is going (which is usually very different from how it ought to go), and what the goal of the battle is." That sergeant gave me an experiential approach to fighting. His three points also provide insight into how experiential religion and preaching ought to go. There are five questions I would like to consider as we address the important subject of Reformed experiential preaching:

What is experiential religion and preaching?

Why is the experiential aspect of preaching necessary?

What are the essential characteristics of experiential preaching?

Why must a minister be experientially prepared

for the ministry?

What practical lessons on Christian living can we learn from the experiential preaching of our predecessors?

Defining Experiential Religion and Preaching

Experiential or experimental preaching addresses the vital matter of how a Christian experiences the truth of Christian doctrine in his life. The term "experimental" comes from the Latin *experimentum*, meaning trial. It is derived from the verb *experior*, meaning "to try, prove, or put to the test." That same verb can also mean "to find or know by experience," thus leading to the word *experientia*, meaning knowledge gained by experiment. John Calvin used experiential and experimental interchangeably, since both words in biblical preaching indicate the need for measuring experienced knowledge against the touchstone of Scripture.

Experimental preaching stresses the need to know by experience the great truths of the Word of God. A working definition of experimental preaching might be: Experimental preaching seeks to explain in terms of biblical truth how matters ought to go, how they do go, and what is the goal of the Christian life. It aims to apply divine truth to the whole range of the believer's personal experience as well as in his relationships with family, the church, and the world around him.

Paul Helm wrote about such preaching: "The situation [today] calls for preaching that will cover the full range of Christian experience, and a developed experimental theology. The preaching must give guidance and instruction to Christians in terms of their actual experience. It must not deal in unrealities or treat congregations as if they lived in a different century or in wholly different circumstances. This involves taking the full measure of our modern situation and entering with full sympathy into the actual experiences, the hopes and fears, of Christian people."[1]

Experimental preaching is discriminatory preaching. It clearly defines the difference between a Christian and non-Christian, opening the kingdom of heaven to one and shutting it against the other. Discriminatory preaching offers the forgiveness of sins and eternal life to all who by a true faith embrace Christ as Savior and Lord, but it also proclaims the wrath of God and His eternal condemnation upon those who are unbelieving, unrepentant, and unconverted. Such preaching teaches that unless our religion is experiential, we will perish—not because experience itself saves, but because the Christ who saves sinners must be experi-

---

[1] "Christian Experience," *Banner of Truth*, No. 139 (April 1975):6.

enced personally as the foundation upon which the house of our eternal hope is built (Matthew 7:22–27; 1 Corinthians 1:30; 2:2).

Experimental preaching is applicatory. It applies the text to every aspect of a listener's life, promoting a religion that is truly a power and not mere form (2 Timothy 3:5). Robert Burns defined such religion as "Christianity brought home to men's business and bosoms," and said the principle on which it rests is "that Christianity should not only be known, and understood, and believed, but also felt, and enjoyed, and practically applied."[2]

Experiential preaching, then, teaches that the Christian faith must be experienced, tasted, and lived through the saving power of the Holy Spirit. It stresses the knowledge of scriptural truth "which is able to make us wise unto salvation through faith in Christ Jesus" (2 Timothy 3:15). Specifically, such preaching teaches that Christ, who is the living Word (John. 1:1) and the very embodiment of the truth, must be experientially known and embraced. It proclaims the need for sinners to experience who God is in His Son. As John 17:3 says, "And this is life eternal, that they might know Thee, the only true God, and Jesus Christ, whom Thou hast sent." The word "know" in this text, as well as other bib-

---

[2] *Works of Thomas Halyburton* (London: Thomas Tegg, 1835), xiv–xv.

lical usages, does not indicate casual acquaintance, but a deep, abiding relationship. For example, Genesis 4:1 uses the word "know" to suggest marital intimacy: "And Adam knew Eve his wife; and she conceived, and bare Cain." Experiential preaching stresses the intimate, personal knowledge of God in Christ.

Such knowledge is never divorced from Scripture. According to Isaiah 8:20, all of our beliefs, including our experiences, must be tested against Holy Scripture. "If I can't find my experiences back in the Bible, they are not from the Lord but from the devil," Martin Luther once said. That is really what the word "experimental," derived from experiment, intends to convey. Just as scientific experiment means testing a hypothesis against a body of evidence, so experimental preaching involves examining experience in the light of the teaching of the Word of God.

Reformed experimental preaching, grounded in the Word of God, is theocentric rather than anthropocentric. Some people accuse the Puritans of being man-centered in their passion for godly experience. But as J. I. Packer argues, the Puritans were not interested in tracing the experience of the Spirit's work in their souls to promote their own experience, but to be driven out of themselves into Christ, in whom they could then enter into fellowship with the Triune God.

This passion for fellowship with the Triune God means that experimental preaching not only addresses the believer's conscience, but also his relationship with others in the church and the world. If experimental preaching led me only to examine my experiences and my relationship with God, it would fall short of affecting my interaction with family, church members, and society. It would then remain self-centered. Rather, true experimental preaching brings a believer into the realm of vital Christian experience, prompting a love for God and His glory as well as a burning passion to declare that love to others around him. A believer so instructed cannot help but be evangelistic since vital experience and a heart for missions are inseparable.

In sum, Reformed experimental preaching addresses the entire range of Christian living. With the Spirit's blessing, its mission is to transform the believer in all that he is and does so that he becomes more and more like the Savior.

Many Reformed ministers preached experimentally until early in the 19th century. Francis Wayland wrote in 1857 in his *Notes on the Principles and Practices of the Baptist Churches*:

> From the manner in which our ministers entered upon the work, it is evident that it must

have been the prominent object of their lives to convert men to God. They were remarkable for what was called experimental preaching. They told much of the exercises of the human soul under the influence of the truth of the gospel. The feeling of a sinner while under the convicting power of the truth; the various subterfuges to which he resorted when aware of his danger; the successive applications of truth by which he was driven out of all of them; the despair of the soul when it found itself wholly without a refuge; its final submission to God, and simple reliance on Christ; the joys of the new birth and the earnestness of the soul to introduce others to the happiness which it has now for the first time experienced; the trials of the soul when it found itself an object of reproach and persecution among those whom it loved best; the process of sanctification; the devices of Satan to lead us into sin; the mode in which the attacks of the adversary may be resisted; the danger of backsliding, with its evidences, and the means of recovery from it . . . these remarks show the tendency of the class of preachers which seem now to be passing away.[3]

How different experiential preaching is from what we so often hear today! The Word of God is

---

[3] Cited in Iain Murray, *Revival and Revivalism* (Edinburgh: Banner of Truth Trust, 1994), 321–22.

too often preached in a way that will not transform listeners because it fails to discriminate and fails to apply. Such preaching is reduced to a lecture, a demonstration, a catering to what people want to hear. Or it is the kind of subjectivism that is divorced from the foundation of Scripture. Such preaching fails to explain from Scripture what the Reformed called "vital religion": how a sinner must be stripped of his righteousness, driven to Christ alone for salvation, and led to the joy of simple reliance upon Christ. It fails to show how a sinner encounters the plague of indwelling sin, battles against backsliding, and gains victory by faith in Christ.

By contrast, when God's Word is preached experimentally, it is "the power of God unto salvation" (Romans 1:16) that transforms men and nations. For such preaching proclaims from the gates of hell, as it were, that those who are not born again will walk through those gates to dwell there eternally unless they repent (Luke 13:1–9). And such preaching proclaims from the gates of heaven that those who by God's grace persevere in holiness will walk through those gates into eternal glory, where they will dwell in unceasing communion with the Triune God.

Such preaching is transforming because it accurately reflects the vital experience of the children of

God (cf. Romans 5:1–11), clearly explains the marks and fruits of the saving grace necessary for a believer (Matthew 5:3–12; Galatian 5:22–23), and sets before believer and unbeliever alike their eternal futures (Revelation 21:1–9).

The Necessity of Experimental Preaching

Preaching today must be experiential for the following reasons:

1. Scripture commands it. Preaching is rooted in grammatical and historical exegesis, but also involves spiritual, practical, and experimental application. In 1 Corinthians 2:10–16, Paul says that good exegesis is spiritual. Since the Spirit always testifies of Jesus Churst, sound exegesis finds Christ not only in the new covenant, but also in the old. As all roads in the ancient world once led to Rome, so the preaching of all texts today must ultimately lead to Christ. Jesus Himself said, "Search the Scriptures; for in them ye think ye have eternal life . . . and they are they which testify of Me" (John 5:39). Likewise, when He spoke with the travelers to Emmaus, Jesus said, "These are the words which I spake unto you while I was yet with you, that all things must be fulfilled which were written in the law of Moses, and in the prophets, and in the psalms, concerning Me" (Luke 24:44). Spiritual exegesis is thus Christological exegesis, and,

through Christ, it will be theological exegesis, bringing all glory to the Triune God.

Exegesis offers sound analysis of the words, grammar, syntax, and the historical setting of Scripture. Experiential preaching does not minimize these aspects of interpretation, but it is not content with them. Words, grammar, syntax, and historical setting serve God in exegeting the Word of God, but they are not enough.

Exposition alone is not preaching. A minister who only presents the grammatical and historical meaning of God's Word may be lecturing or discoursing, but he isn't preaching. The Word must also be applied. This application is an essential characteristic of Reformed preaching. Without it, vitality is quenched.

Jesus shows us how to preach experientially in the Sermon on the Mount. He begins the sermon by explaining who are true citizens of the kingdom of heaven through the beatitudes, which also are a beautiful summary of the Christian experience. The first three beatitudes (spiritual poverty, mourning, and meekness) focus on the inward disposition of the believer, the fourth (hungering and thirsting after righteousness) reveals the heartbeat of experiential faith, and the last four (merciful, pure in heart, peacemakers, and persecuted) show faith in the midst of the world. The beatitudes thus reveal the marks of genuine piety. The remainder of Jesus' sermon shows the fruits of grace in a believer's life.

2. True religion is more than notion. Because true religion is experimental, preaching must relate to the vital experience of the children of God. Consider the experience of affliction. Romans 5:3–5 says, "We glory in tribulations also: knowing that tribulation worketh patience; and patience, experience; and experience, hope: and hope maketh not ashamed." In this passage, Paul regards experience as an important link to the blessings that flow out of sanctified affliction.

Paul's epistles are filled with experiential truth. Romans 7, for example, shows that human depravity forces a believer to groan, "Oh, wretched man that I am!" and Romans 8 leads a believer to the heights of divine riches in Christ, which the Spirit reveals in all its comfort and glory. Paul concludes by saying that nothing we experience in this life can separate believers from the love of God in Christ Jesus.

Experiential preaching shows the comfort of the living church and the glory of God. How could a minister preach the opening words of Isaiah 40 without an experiential emphasis? " 'Comfort ye, comfort ye my people,' saith your God. Speak ye comfortably to Jerusalem, and cry unto her, that her warfare is accomplished, that her iniquity is pardoned: for she hath received of the Lord's hand double for all her sins" (vv. 1–2). A nonexperiential sermon fails to offer life and power and comfort to the believer. It also fails to glorify God as Isaiah so elequently does in the remainder of the chapter.

3. Without such preaching, we will everlastingly perish. Experience itself does not save. We cannot have faith in our experience or faith in our faith. Our faith is in Christ alone, but that faith is experiential. Unless we build on the Rock of Christ Jesus (Matthew 7:22–27), our house of hope will crash. Some preachers may not know what it means personally, vitally, and experientially to build upon that Rock. Yet if they are to lead others to Christ, they above all must understand experientially what Paul declares in 1 Corinthians: "But of Him [God the Father] are ye in Christ Jesus, who of God is made unto us wisdom, and righteousness, and sanctification, and redemption. . . . For I determined not to know anything among you, save Jesus Christ, and Him crucified" (1:30; 2:2).

The Characteristics of Experiential Preaching

Experiential preaching includes the following characteristics:

1. God's Word is central in it. Preaching flows out of the scriptural passage that is expounded in accord with sound exegetical and hermeneutical

principles. As Jeremiah 3:15 says, God has given preachers to His church to "feed them with knowledge and understanding." Proper preaching does not add an experiential part to the text being preached; rather, with the Spirit's light, it draws the true experience of believers from the text. The minister must bring the sincere milk of the Word in order that, by the Spirit's blessing, experiential preaching will foster true growth (1 Peter 2:2; Romans 10:14).

Centering on the Word preserves experiential preaching from unbiblical mysticism. Mysticism separates experience from the Word of God, whereas historic Reformed conviction demands Word-centered, God-glorifying, Spirit-wrought, experiential Christianity. That kind of preaching is essential to the health and prosperity of the church. As Calvin says, God begets and multiplies His church only by means of His Word (James 1:18).

2. It is discerning. A faithful minister rightly divides the Word of truth to separate the precious from the vile (Jeremiah 15:19), emphasizing law and gospel as well as death in Adam and life in Christ for that purpose. Grace is to be offered indiscriminately to all (Matthew 13:24–30); however, the divine acts, marks, and fruits of grace that God works in His people must be explained to encourage the elect and uncover the false hopes of the

hypocrite.

Biblical experiential preaching stresses what God does in, for, and through His elect. As Philippians 2:13 says, "For it is God which worketh in you both to will and to do of His good pleasure." Expounding the divine acts, marks, and fruits of grace is critical in our day when so much that is man-glorifying passes for genuine Christianity. We must preach about the fruits of grace that distinguish true belief from counterfeit Christianity. We must be obedient to 2 Corinthians 13:5, which says, "Examine yourselves, whether ye be in the faith; prove your own selves," as well as to James 2:17, which says, "Faith, if it hath not works, is dead, being alone."

3. It explains how things go in the lives of God's people and how they ought to go (Romans 7–8). Telling how matters go without indicating how they should go lulls the believer into ceasing from pressing on in his spiritual pilgrimage. He will not press forward to grow in the grace and knowledge of Christ (2 Peter 3:18). Telling how matters should be rather than how they are discourages the believer from being assured that the Lord has ever worked in his heart. He may fear that the marks and fruits of grace are too high for him to claim. The true believer thus needs to hear both. He must be encouraged in spite of all his infirmities not to

despair for Christ's sake (Hebrews 4:15). He must also be warned against assuming that he has reached the end of his spiritual pilgrimage and be urged to "press toward the mark for the prize of the high calling of God in Christ Jesus" (Philippians 3:14).

Every Christian is a fighting soldier. To win the war against evil, a believer must put on the whole armor of God (Ephesians 6:10–20). Experiential preaching brings the believer to the battlefield, shows him how to fight, tells him how to win and lose skirmishes, and reminds him of the victory that awaits him in which God will receive the glory. "For of Him, and through Him, and to Him are all things, to whom be glory forever. Amen" (Romans 11:36).

4. It stresses inward knowledge. The old divines were fond of stressing the difference between head knowledge and heart knowledge in Christian faith. Head knowledge is not enough for true religion; it also demands heart knowledge. "Keep thy heart with all diligence; for out of it are the issues of life," says Proverbs 4:23. Romans 10:10 adds, "For with the heart man believeth unto righteousness."

To illustrate, consider the minister who went to a Christian bookstore where a book he had written was being sold. The storekeeper asked the minister whether he knew the book's author. When the man

said yes, the storekeeper said that he was also ac-
quainted with the author. The minister disputed
that. The storekeeper looked puzzled and asked
why he was being questioned. The minister replied,
"Sir, if you knew the author, you would have
greeted me as such when I entered your store!"

The storekeeper's acquaintance with the author
was mere head knowledge. Despite his claims, he
did not truly know the author; he didn't even recognize the man when he met him. His knowledge
of the author was not experiential; it was not the
fruit of personal communion with the author. It
lacked the kind of heart knowledge that would
have made it authentic.

Heart knowledge of God in Christ results from a
personal, experiential encounter with Christ
through the wondrous work of the Spirit. Such
knowledge transforms the heart and bears heavenly
fruit. It savors the Lord and delights in Him (Job
34:9; Psalm 34:7; Isaiah 58:14). It tastes and sees
that God in Christ loves lost, depraved, hell-worthy
sinners (Psalm 34:8). Heart knowledge includes an
appetite for tasting and digesting God's truth. As
Jeremiah says, "Thy words were found, and I did
eat them; and Thy word was unto me the joy and
rejoicing of mine heart" (Jeremiah 15:16). Heart
knowledge feasts on God, His Word, His truth,
and His Son (Psalm 144:15; 146:5).

Heart knowledge does not lack head knowledge, but head knowledge may lack heart knowledge (Romans 10:8–21). Some people pursue religion as an objective study or to appease their conscience, without ever allowing it to penetrate their
heart. They have never become guilty and condemned before the holy justice of God. They have
not experienced deliverance in Christ so they are
unaware of the kind of gratitude for such deliverance that masters a believer's soul, mind, and
strength. By contrast, those who experience saving
heart knowledge find sin such an unbearable burden that Christ is altogether necessary. The grace of
deliverance through the Savior is then so over-
whelming that their lives shine forth with gratitude.

Head knowledge is not evil in and of itself. Most
of our Reformed and Puritan forefathers were
highly educated. The Reformers never tired of
stressing the value of Christian education. But this
education must be empowered by the Holy Spirit
and applied to the heart. Head knowledge is insuf-
ficient without the Spirit's application to the inward man.

5. It must be centered in Jesus Christ (John 1:29,
36). According to 1 Corinthians 2:2, a true preacher
must be "determined not to know anything . . . save
Jesus Christ, and Him crucified." Or, as William
Perkins once said, the heart of all preaching is "to

preach one Christ, by Christ, to the praise of Christ."[4]

Christ must be the beginning, middle, and end of every sermon (Luke 24:27; Acts 5:5, 35; 1 John 1:1–4). Preaching must exalt Christ for awakening, justifying, sanctifying, and comforting sinners (Ephesians 5:4; 1 Corinthians 1:30; Isaiah 61:2). As John says, "In Him was life; and the life was the light of men. . . . The word was made flesh, and dwelt among us, and we beheld His glory, the glory as of the only begotten of the Father, full of grace and truth" (John 1:4, 14; cf. Psalm 36:9; 119:130).

Experiential preaching must stress what Rowland Hill calls the "three R's" of preaching: Ruin by the fall, Righteousness by Christ, and Regeneration by the Spirit. Experience does not save the sinner, but Christ saves in an experiential way (Philippians 1:6). Christ is the divine fulcrum upon which genuine experience pivots.

Experiential preaching teaches that a Christian must not be separated from Christ. Though conviction of sin cannot save us, it is nonetheless critical. Under the Spirit's tutelage, conviction of sin and misery lead us to the Savior, where we cry out, "Give me Jesus else I die." As Martin Luther once said, "Being saved is going lost at Jesus' feet."

---

[4] *Works of William Perkins* (London: John Legatt, 1613), 2:762.

6. Its aim is to glorify the Triune God: the Father's eternal love and good pleasure, Christ's redemptive and mediatorial work, and the Spirit's sanctifying and preserving ministry. The minister's goal in preaching is to help people fall in love with each person of the Trinity. As Samuel Rutherford said, "I know not which divine person I love the most, but this I know, I need and love each of them."

Experiential preaching stresses the God-centered nature of each benefit of salvation: internal calling, regeneration, faith, justification, sanctification, and perseverance. Experiential preaching differentiates between what is of man and what is of God. It exalts what is of God and abases what is of man (John 3:30).

Let us seek grace daily to experience the saving work of the Triune God. We can offer no better petition than the simple prayer of Moses, "Show me now Thy way, that I may know Thee" (Exodus 33:13b). Or, as Sukey Harley prayed, "Lord, make me to know myself; make me to know Thyself." Knowing the Triune God is the marrow of genuine Christian experience (cf. Jeremiah 9:23–24; John 17:3).

Preparation for the Ministry

It is impossible to separate godly, experiential

living from true experiential ministry. The sanctification of a minister's heart is not merely ideal; it is absolutely necessary both personally and for his calling as a minister of the gospel.

Scripture says there should be no disparity between the heart, character, and life of a man who is called to proclaim God's Word, and the content of the message he proclaims. "Take heed unto thyself, and unto the doctrine; continue in them; for in doing this thou shalt both save thyself, and them that hear thee" (1 Timothy 4:16).

Jesus condemned the Pharisees and scribes for not doing what they proclaimed. He faulted them for the difference that existed between their words and deeds, between what they professionally proclaimed and how they acted in their daily life. Professional clerics, more than anyone else, should consider the scathing words of Christ: "The scribes and the Pharisees sit in Moses' seat. All therefore whatsoever they bid you observe, that observe and do; but do not ye after their works: for they say, and do not" (Matthew 23:2–3). As ministers, we are called to be as holy in our private relationship with God, in our role as husbands and fathers at home, and as shepherds among our people as we appear to be on the pulpit. There must be no disjunction between our calling and our living, between our confession and practice.

Scripture says there is a cause-and-effect relationship between the character of a man's life as a Christian and his fruitfulness as a minister (Matthew 7:17–20). A minister's work is usually blessed in proportion to the sanctification of his heart before God. Ministers must therefore seek grace to build the house of God with sound experiential preaching and doctrine as well as with a sanctified life. Our preaching must shape our life, and our life must adorn our preaching. As John Boys wrote, "He doth preach most who doth live best."

We must be what we preach, not only applying ourselves to our texts but applying our texts to ourselves. Our hearts must be transcripts of our sermons.[5] Otherwise, as John Owen warned, "If a man teach uprightly and walk crookedly, more will fall down in the night of his life than he built in the day of his doctrine."

Lessons from the Experiential Preachers

The old experimental preachers were masters at applying truth to their own hearts as well as to those of others. Here are some lessons from the divines that will serve us well today.

1. Live close to God. You can't fake Reformed,

---

[5] Gardiner Spring, *The Power of the Pulpit* (reprint, Edinburgh: Banner of Truth Trust, 1986), 154.

experiential living any more than you can fake Reformed, experiential preaching. As people see through ministers who try to preach experientially, but don't live up to what they preach, so we must live close to God in order to show others that Christianity is real and experiential. For our words and actions to convey godly piety, our very thoughts must pulsate with that piety which only flows out of a close life with God. "As a man thinketh, so is he."

2. Pursue godliness in dependence on the Holy Spirit. The way to godly living is surprisingly simple: We are to walk with God in His appointed way (Micah 6:8), diligently using the means of grace and the spiritual disciplines, and waiting upon the Holy Spirit for blessing. Note that godly living involves both discipline and grace. This emphasis upon duty and grace is fundamental to Reformed, experiential thinking on godly living.[6] As John Flavel wrote, "The duty is ours, though the power be God's. A natural man has no power, a gracious man hath some, though not sufficient; and that power he hath depends upon the assist-

---

[6] Daniel Webber, "Sanctifying the Inner Life," in *Aspects of Sanctification, 1981 Westminster Conference Papers* (Hertfordshire: Evangelical Press, 1982), 44–45.

ing strength of Christ."[7]

Likewise, John Owen wrote, "It is the Holy Ghost who is the immediate peculiar sanctifier of all believers, and the author of all holiness in them. The Spirit supplies what we lack so that we may press toward the mark of holiness, enabling us as believers to yield obedience to God . . . by virtue of the life and death of Jesus Christ."[8]

The believer then is empowered, as Flavel said, with "a diligent and constant use and improvement of all holy means and duties, to preserve the soul from sin, and maintain its sweet and free communion with God."[9] We can also be encouraged by Owen's advice: "If thou meanest to enlarge thy religion, do it rather by enlarging thy ordinary devotions than thy extraordinary."

Reformed experiential preachers frequently advised listeners to exercise spiritual disciplines that would promote experiential and practical Christian living. Specifically they advised:

• Read Scripture diligently and meditatively (1 Timothy 4:13). Richard Greenham said that we ought to read our Bibles with more diligence than

---

[7] *The Works of John Flavel* (reprint, London: Banner of Truth Trust, 1968), 5:424.

[8] *The Works of John Owen* (reprint ,Edinburgh: Banner of Truth Trust, 1976), 3:385–86.

[9] *Works of Flavel*, 5:423.

men dig for hidden treasure. Diligence makes the rough places plain, the difficult easy, and the unsavory tasty.[10]

After reading Scripture, we must ask God for light to scrutinize our hearts and lives, then meditate upon the Word. Disciplined meditation on Scripture helps us focus on God. Meditation helps us view worship as a discipline. It involves our mind and understanding as well as our heart and affections. It works Scripture through the texture of the soul. Meditation helps prevent vain and sinful thoughts (Matthew 12:35) and provides inner resources on which to draw (Psalm 77:10–12), including direction for daily life (Proverbs 6:21–22). Meditation fights temptation (Psalm 119:11, 15), provides relief in afflictions (Isaiah 49:15–17), benefits others (Psalm 145:7), and glorifies God (Psalm 49:3).

• Pray without ceasing. We must sustain the habit of secret prayer if we are to live experientially before God. The only way to learn the art of holy argument with God is to pray. Prayer helps us cling to the altar of God's promises by which we lay hold of God Himself.

---

[10] *The Works of the Reverend and Faithfvll Servant of Iesvs Christ, M. Richard Greenham,* ed. H[enry] H[olland] (London: Felix Kingston for Robert Dexter, 1599), 390.

Failing to pray is the downfall of many Christians today. "A family without prayer is like a house without a roof, open and exposed to all the storms of heaven," wrote Thomas Brooks. If the giants of church history dwarf us today, perhaps it is not because they were more educated, more devout, or more faithful as much as because they were men of prayer. They were possessed with the Spirit of supplication. They were Daniels in the temple of God.

Let us cling to the refuge of the inner prayer chamber, for here experiential Christianity is either established or broken. Let us refuse to be content with the shell of religion without the inner core of prayer. When we grow drowsy in prayer, let us pray aloud, or write down our prayers, or find a quiet place outside to walk and pray. Above all, let us continue to pray.

We should not give up regular times of prayer, but we should also be open to prayer at the slightest impulse to do so. Conversing with God through Christ is our most effective antidote to spiritual backsliding and discouragement. Discouragement without prayer is an open sore ripe for infection, whereas discouragement with prayer is a sore lifted to the balm of Gilead.

Keep prayer a priority in your personal and family life. As John Bunyan said, "You can do more than pray after you have prayed, but you cannot do more than pray until you have prayed. Pray often, for prayer is a shield to the soul, a sacrifice to God, and a scourge to Satan."[11]

• Study Reformed experiential literature. Books that promote godly living are a powerful aid to experiential living. Read the spiritual classics, inviting great writers to be your spiritual mentors and friends. The Puritans excel in such writing. "There must scarcely be a sermon, a treatise, a pamphlet, a diary, a history, or a biography from a Puritan pen, which was not in one way or another aimed at fostering the spiritual life," said Maurice Roberts.[12]

Read sound experiential books on various topics to meet a variety of needs. To foster experiential living by remaining sensitized to sin, read Ralph Venning's *The Plague of Plagues* (Banner of Truth) or Jeremiah Burroughs's *The Evil of Evils* (Soli Deo Gloria). To be drawn closer to Christ, read Isaac Ambrose's *Looking Unto Jesus* (Sprinkle Publications). To find peace in affliction, read Samuel Rutherford's *Letters*. To gain relief from

---

[11] *Prayer* (reprint, Edinburgh: Banner of Truth Trust, 1999), 23ff.

[12] "Visible Saints: The Puritans as a Godly People," in *Aspects of Sanctification, 1981 Westminster Conference Papers* (Hertfordshire: Evangelical Press, 1982), 1–2.

temptation, read John Owen's *Temptation and Sin* (Banner of Truth). To grow in holiness, read John Flavel's *Keeping the Heart* (Soli Deo Gloria).

Read as an act of worship. Read to be elevated into the great truths of God so that you may worship the Trinity in Spirit and in truth. Be selective about what you read, however. Measure all your reading against the touchstone of Scripture. So much of today's Christian literature is froth, riddled with Arminian theology or secular thinking. Time is too precious to waste on nonsense. Read more for eternity than time, more for spiritual growth than professional advancement. Think of John Trapp's warning: "As water tastes of the soil it runs through, so does the soul taste of the authors that a man reads."

Before picking up a book, ask yourself: Would Christ approve of this book? Will it increase my love for the Word of God, help me to conquer sin, offer abiding wisdom, and prepare me for the life to come? Or could I better spend time reading another book?

Speak to others about the good books that you read. Conversation about experiential reading promotes experiential living.

• Make right use of the sacraments. God's sacraments complement His Word. Each sign—water, bread, and wine—nourishes belief in Christ and His sacrifice on the cross, which is the basis for experiential living. The sacraments are visible means through which we and Christ commune. They encourage us to be like Christ in all His holiness.

The grace received through the sacraments is no different from that received through the Word. Both convey the same Christ. But as Robert Bruce put it, "While we do not get a better Christ in the sacraments than in the Word, sometimes we get Christ better."[13]

• Commune with believers. "As the communion of saints is in our creed, so it should be in our company," wrote Thomas Watson. That's good advice. The church ought to be a fellowship of caring as well as a community of prayer (1 Corinthians 12:7; Acts 2:42). So talk and pray with believers whose godly walk you admire (Colossians 3:16). Association promotes assimilation. A Christian who lives in isolation from other believers will fail to receive the blessings as well as the maturity resulting from godly interaction.[14]

• Keep a journal. Keeping a thoughtful record of

---

[13] Read Westminster's *Larger Catechism*, Questions 161–175, for how to use the sacraments properly.

[14] Joel R. Beeke, *Assurance of Faith: Calvin, English Puritanism, and the Dutch Second Reformation* (New York: Peter Lang, 1991), 407–408.

your spiritual journey can promote godliness. It
can help us in our meditation and prayer. It can
remind us of the Lord's faithfulness and work. It
can help us understand and evaluate ourselves. It
can help us monitor our goals and priorities as
well as maintain other spiritual disciplines.[15]

• Keep the Lord's Day holy. We ought to view
the Sabbath as a joyful privilege, not as a tedious
burden. This is the day on which we may worship
God and practice spiritual disciplines without in-
terruption. As J. I. Packer says, "We are to rest from
the business of our earthly calling in order to pros-
ecute the business of our heavenly calling."[16]

• Serve others and tell them about Christ. Jesus
expects us to evangelize and serve others (Matthew
28:19–20; Hebrews 9:14). We are to do so out of
obedience (Deuteronomy 13:4), gratitude (1 Samuel
12:24), gladness (Psalm 100:2), humility (John
13:15–16), and love (Galatians 5:13). Serving others
may be difficult at times, but we are called to do so,
using every spiritual gift that God has granted us

---

[15] Donald S. Whitney, *Spiritual Disciplines for the Christian Life*
(Colorado Springs: NavPress, 1991), 196–210.
[16] *A Quest for Godliness: The Puritan Vision of the Christian Life*
(Wheaton, Ill: Crossway Books, 1990), 239; Errol Hulse,
"Sanctifying the Lord's Day: Reformed and Puritan Atti-
tudes," in *Aspects of Sanctification, 1981 Westminster Conference Papers* (Hertfordshire: Evangelical Press, 1982), 78–102.

(cf. Romans 12:4–8; 1 Corinthians 12:6–11; Ephesians 4:7–13). One of our greatest rewards as Christians is to serve people. If the result is watching them draw closer to Christ through the Spirit's blessing upon God's Word and our efforts, what more could we possibly ask for? It is a profoundly humbling experience that can only draw us closer to God.

3. Aim for balanced thinking. The great Reformed experiential preachers aimed for balance in Christian living in three important ways:

• Between the objective and subjective dimensions of Christianity. The objective is the food for the subjective; thus the subjective is always rooted in the objective. For example, the Puritans stated that the primary ground of assurance is rooted in the promises of God, but those promises must become increasingly real to the believer through the subjective evidences of grace and the internal witness of the Holy Spirit. Without the Spirit's application, the promises of God lead to self-deceit and carnal presumption. On the other hand, without the promises of God and the illumination of the Spirit, self-examination tends to introspection, bondage, and legalism. Objective and subjective Christianity must not be separated from each other.

We must seek to live in a way that reveals Christ's internal presence based on His objective work of active and passive obedience. The gospel of Christ must be proclaimed as objective truth, but it must also be applied by the Holy Spirit and inwardly appropriated by faith. We therefore reject two kinds of religion: one that separates subjective experience from the the objective Word, thereby leading to man-centered mysticism; and one that presumes salvation on the false grounds of historical or temporary faith.[17]

• Between the sovereignty of God and the responsibility of man. Nearly all of our Reformed forefathers stressed that God is fully sovereign and man is fully responsible. How that can be resolved logically is beyond our finite minds. When Spurgeon was once asked how these two grand, biblical doctrines could be reconciled, he responded, "I didn't know that friends needed reconciliation."

He went on to compare these two doctrines to the rails of a track upon which Christianity runs. Just as the rails of a train, which run parallel to each other, appear to merge in the distance, so the doctrines of God's sovereignty and man's responsibility, which seem separate from each other in this life will merge in eternity. Our task is not to force

---

[17] Joel R. Beeke, *Quest for Full Assurance: The Legacy of Calvin and His Successors* (Edinburgh: Banner of Truth Trust, 1999), 125, 130, 146.

their merging in this life but to keep them in balance and to live accordingly. We must thus strive for experiential Christianity that does justice both to God's sovereignty and to our responsibility.

• Between doctrinal, experiential, and practical Christianity. Just as Reformed preachers taught that experiential preaching must offer a balance of doctrine and application, Christian living also involves more than experience. Biblical Christian living is grounded in sound doctrine, sound experience, and sound practice.

4. Communicate experiential truth to others. Reformed experiential preachers applied their sermons to every part of life. They applied all of Scripture to the entire man. They were unashamedly doctrinal. We can learn much from them on how to evangelize, such as:

• Speak the truth about God. That seems obvious. But how often do we speak to others about God's majestic being, His Trinitarian personality, and His glorious attributes? How often do we tell others about His holiness, sovereignty, mercy, and love? Do we root our evangelism in a robust biblical theism, or do we take our cues from modern evangelism which approaches God as if He were a next-door neighbor who adjusts His attributes to our needs and desires? How often do we speak to others about how God and His majestic attributes have become experientially real to us?

• Speak the truth about man. Do you talk to others about our depraved nature and our desperate need for salvation in Jesus Christ? Do you say that you are no better than they are by nature; that we are all, apart from grace, sinners with a terrible record, which is a legal problem, as well as a bad heart, which is a moral problem? Do you talk to them about the dreadful character of sin; that sin is something that stems back to our tragic fall in Adam and affects every part of us, so dominating our mind, heart, will, and conscience that we are slaves to it? Do you describe sin as moral rebellion against God? Do you say that the wages of sin is death, now and for all eternity?

• Speak the truth about Christ. Do we present the complete Christ to sinners, not separating His benefits from His person or offering Him as a Savior while ignoring His claims as Lord? Do we offer Christ as the grand remedy for the great malady of sin and repeatedly declare His ability, willingness to save, and preciousness as the exclusive Redeemer of lost sinners?

Do you exhibit the way of salvation in Christ in your faith and repentance? Paul said, "I testified to you publicly and from house to house repentance toward God, and faith toward our Lord Jesus Christ" (Acts 20:20–21). Do you likewise evangelize your friends and neighbors when God offers that opportunity? Do you explain to them what faith and repentance are in a born-again sinner?

• Speak the truth about sanctification. Do you tell others how a Christian must walk the King's highway of holiness in gratitude, service, obedience, love, and self-denial? Do you tell how he must learn the art of meditation, of fearing God, and of childlike prayer? How he must press on by God's grace, seeking to make his calling and election sure? Do you disciple your associates in the need for habitual, experiential faith, repentance, and godliness?[18]

• Speak the truth about eternal consequences. Do not be afraid to speak about the consequences of despising the blood of Jesus Christ. Do not flinch from describing damnation and hell. As one Puritan wrote, "We must go with the stick of divine truth and beat every bush behind which a sinner hides, until, like Adam who hid, he stands before God in his nakedness."

We must speak urgently to people around us because many are on their way to hell. We must confront sinners with the law and gospel, with death in Adam and life in Christ. Let us use every

---

[18] Joel R. Beeke, *Puritan Evangelism: A Biblical Approach* (Grand Rapids, Mich.: Reformation Heritage Books, 1999), 15-16.

weapon we can to turn sinners from the road of
destruction so that they may, though grace, experience a living, experiential relationship with God in
Jesus Christ. We know from Scripture and by experience that an omnipotent Christ can bless our
efforts and rescue a dead sinner, divorce him from
his sinful lusts, and make him willing to forsake
his wicked ways and turn to God, fully resolved to
make God his goal and his praise. Acts 5:31 says,
"Him hath God exalted with His right hand to be a
Prince and a Savior, for to give repentance to Israel,
and forgiveness of sins." Praise God for the
experience of His amazing grace toward us in
Christ!

The Teaching Preacher

R. C. Sproul

In the mid-20th century a full-length film was made on the life of Martin Luther. It included a scene that I found particularly provocative. The action took place after Luther's historic meeting with the authorities of the Holy Roman Empire and of the church at the Diet of Worms. When Luther was called upon to recant of his teachings, he made his epic stand, stating, "Unless I am convinced by sacred Scripture or by evident reason, I cannot recant, for my conscience is held captive by the Word of God; and to act against conscience is neither right nor safe. Here I stand. I can do no other. God help me." He left the assembly hall and was taken on horseback by his friends so that he could be hidden and protected from the authorities who were soon to put a price on his head. They whisked Luther away to the Wartburg Castle. There he grew a beard, and was disguised as a knight known as Sir George. While he was concealed, he set to work on the task of translating the Bible into German. While Luther was hidden away in the castle, his colleague, Carlstadt, in his zeal to promote the Reformation, went to churches and smashed stained glass windows, destroying the art in the churches that had been Roman Catholic, and carried out a reckless work of vandalism in the name of reformation. When word got back to Luther of Carlstadt's destructive activity, he was horrified. This was not what Luther intended by the Reformation. At this time Luther was wanted dead or alive. Nevertheless, he got on his horse, left the castle and came back to the church in Wittenberg. The scene in the movie has Melanchthon and Carlstadt and others meeting quietly behind closed doors. Suddenly, there in chain mail, disguised as a knight, was Martin Luther. They looked at him and said, "Brother Martin, what are you doing? Why are you here?" Luther replied, "I want my pulpit."

What thrilled me about that moment—and I don't know whether that event actually took place in church history or whether this was the license of Hollywood in producing this film—was that it captured the spirit of Luther. One of the most significant things about Luther is that after the Reformation began and Luther was a celebrity throughout Western Europe, he did not spend the ensuing years traveling through Europe trying to consolidate the movement. Rather he returned to the primary vocation to which he had been ordained. He spent his years teaching and preaching in Wittenberg, just as Calvin in Switzerland spent his years preaching in the church and teaching several times each week until the day he died. So when Martin Luther writes and comments on what a preacher should be, and what the task of preaching is in the church, I listen, and I think we all can be instructed from his insights.

One of the great gifts to the church is a large book entitled *What Luther Says* (Concordia House, St. Louis, Mo., 1994). The whole corpus of Luther's *Works* is fifty-some thick volumes, so I take advantage of this anthology where I can look at it topically. In this book Concordia House has collected statements from the various works of Luther regarding the preacher and preaching. What follows is the distilled essence of that collection.

The first thing that is required of a preacher is that he is "apt to teach." At this point Luther is simply echoing the apostolic qualifications set forth in the New Testament for the position of the elder. That person who is elevated to a position of leadership in the church of God, and is given oversight and supervision over the flock of God, must be able to teach. Luther saw this as the primary task of the minister. This concept is all but lost in the church today. When we call ministers to our churches, we demand of them that they be administrators, skilled at fund-raising, and that they are organizers. We also hope that they might know a little bit of theology and a little bit of the Bible, and we expect them to preach interesting and often entertaining sermons. But we don't make it a priority that these people be equipped to teach the congregation the things of God. Luther said that is the primary task of the pastor, of the shepherd, to teach the people of God the things of God.

Think of the encounter that Jesus had with Peter after the resurrection, following Peter's denial of Jesus publicly three times. Jesus confronted Simon Peter and said to him, "Simon, do you love Me?"

Peter responded, "Lord, you know that I love you."

And Jesus said, "Then feed My lambs."

"Peter," for the second time He asked, "do you love Me?"

Peter perhaps manifested a little annoyance that Jesus would ask him this again, "Lord, you know that I love you!"

"Then feed my sheep. Peter, do you love Me?"

"Yes, Lord. You know that I love you."

"Then tend My sheep."

Three times Jesus instructs the apostle to be engaged in the tending and caring, the leading and the feeding of His sheep. It is because the people of God who are assembled in the congregations of the churches all over America belong to Jesus; they are

His sheep. Every minister who is ordained is consecrated and entrusted by God with the care of those sheep. That is why we call the position "the pastorate," or "the pastoral ministry," because we care for the sheep of Christ. And what shepherd would so neglect his sheep that he never took time or the trouble to feed them? It is the feeding of the sheep, according to Luther, that is the number one task of the ministry. And that feeding comes, principally, through teaching.

I make a distinction between preaching—which involves exhortation, exposition, admonition, encouragement, and comfort—and teaching, which involves the transfer of information and instruction in various things of content. There is a difference between teaching and preaching, and I have both of those enterprises in my life. But sometimes I obscure the distinction. The students in my seminary classes will testify that sometimes, in the middle of my lectures, when I'm trying to communicate certain doctrines and information about theology, I'll get to preaching, because I'm not interested just in transferring information. I want that information not only to get in their heads, but to get in their bloodstreams. I warn them at the beginning: "Don't think that I'm in this classroom as a professor in a state of neutrality. I'm after your mind. I want not only to instruct you, I want to persuade you. I want to move you to grasp not only the truth of this content, but also the importance and the sweetness of it, so that you will take it with you for the rest of your lives. I'm not interested in transfering information from me to your notebook, and from your notebook to the shelf, because learning doesn't take place until it gets in your head and into your life."

My whole life has been dedicated to teaching; but sometimes, when I'm teaching, I preach. And when I preach, I will often sprinkle some conceptual education into the content of my sermons. So I have a tendency to skate back and forth across the line between preaching and teaching. But I've always thought that the number one thing, as Luther understood, that I'm responsible to do as a minister is to teach the people the things of God. Luther was teaching the people of Wittenberg almost on a daily basis, as Calvin was in Geneva, for they understood that the task of learning for a Christian is a lifelong enterprise.

And here we may well ask Luther, if the number one priority of the minister is that he is able to teach, then what is he to teach? What Luther said was to teach the Bible, the content of Scripture. John Calvin wrote a commentary on almost every book of the Bible, and those commentaries grew out of his teaching seminars with his congregation in Geneva, Switzerland. Luther also wrote much in the way of commentaries that he took from his lectures to the people and to the students at Wittenberg to instruct them in sacred Scripture.

At the present, I teach systematic theology and apologetics at Knox Seminary in Ft. Lauderdale, Florida. A few years ago as a faculty we reviewed our curriculum and we began to tinker with it a bit. We asked ourselves: what does a man have to know in order to be a godly pastor? So we began to develop a curriculum from ground zero. We said, let's step out of the academic world for a minute and design the curriculum here not so the professors can be fulfilled in the areas of their specialties, but so that we can understand our task as serving the church and thereby serving Christ. This was the historic role of the seminary: to be a servant of Christ by equipping men to be pastors in the church—not to be theological universities where people could get academic credentials. There is a place for that, but when we started looking at what seminary graduates needed to know, we decided that the number one thing is the content of Holy Scripture. We declared, there's not enough time in three years to teach students church history, theology, Old Testament and New Testament, so we considered changing the curriculum into a four or even a five-year program. But we were dissuaded from that, knowing that no one would come, because everyone else can get their degree in a three-year program. I know of seminaries where a person can get a degree to become a minister and not have a single course in Bible content. So many of our courses in the seminary are designed to answer academic questions of background, of authorship and life situation and technical problems, so that we never get around to the English Bible. Our future ministers are coming out of seminaries not fully conversant with the content of the Bible. The last people in the world the pastors want to find out about that are their congregations.

So many ministers are frankly afraid to teach the content of Scripture to the people because they haven't learned it themselves first. The people of God need to say to their pastors, or to their prospective pastors, "Feed us the Word of God." Be careful to choose a pastor who will open up the Scriptures to you.

The last months of the year 2000 were a period of mourning for me over the loss of one of my closest friends and comrades in the ministry, Dr. James Montgomery Boice. Jim Boice represented to me the model minister. Here is a man who went to Harvard University for his undergraduate degree, then to Princeton Seminary for his degree for ministry, and from there to the University of Basil in Switzerland for his doctor's degree in New

Testament study. Jim Boice had all the academic credentials a person could ever want to go to the top of the ladder in the academic world, but that was not his call. His call was to be a pastor. For over thirty years he broke open the Word of God in his preaching, in his teaching, and in his writings. Fidelity to Scripture is what drove him, and a more courageous Christian I have never met. Pastoral ministry, the teaching of the Word, is what God expects from those whom He sets apart and ordains as ministers. He desires that they will take His Word and give it to the people.

Of course pastors are expected, according to Luther, to manifest a godly life. Yet, when Luther considered what it was to have a godly life, he wasn't talking simply about moral virtue. Above all things the pastor, in his doctrine, must be irreproachable. In the 16th century, it was said of the difference between Erasmus—with his satirical book attacking the corruption of the clergy entitled *The Praise of Folly*—and Luther, who was his contemporary, that Erasmus attacked the pope in his belly and Luther attacked him in his doctrine. But Luther wasn't interested in doctrine removed from life. For Luther, doctrine *is* life, because what a person believes is what determines his behavior. That's why he said that the minister must be irreproachable in his doctrine, that that preacher who preaches the Word of God must be sound in his understanding of the sacred Scriptures.

One of the things that came out of the Protestant Reformation was a major change in church architecture. In the medieval Catholic church, the center of the sanctuary, the focal point, was the altar, because it was there the sacrament of the Lord's Supper was celebrated in every mass. So the whole emphasis was on the sacerdotal or priestly function that was communicated through the sacraments. The pulpits were generally off to the side and were not that important to Sunday morning worship. But once the Reformation came into the church, the architecture began to change. The pulpit now was moved to the center of the sanctuary and the worship service began to focus on preaching. Luther and Calvin (and John Knox in Scotland) were all responsible contributors to this shift in emphasis of worship.

Again, Luther saw teaching and preaching as the primary task of the ministry. He said that the minister, or the preacher in this case, needed to be sure of his doctrine. That is a strange quality for a great minister. In this day and age we tend to put a premium on openness, and we don't like a dogmatic spirit where people are too certain of that which they teach or preach. We almost expect the minister, if he is to be politically correct, to say,

"Well maybe it is this and maybe it is that," because we don't want the minister to offend anybody
by a proclamation that communicates too much
certainty or authority. But Luther said "No, no, no,
no." The pastor is responsible to do his homework.
He's not supposed to manifest the certitude that is
born of arrogance, but rather the certainty that
comes from the text of Scripture itself.

A debate took place in the 16th century between
Erasmus and Luther. At the beginning of the
Reformation Erasmus applauded Luther. He was a
fan and encouraged Luther, but he soon felt that
Luther went way too far. Erasmus soon emerged as
one of Luther's chief critics. He wrote his scathing
critique of Luther in his book entitled *The Diatribe*.
Perhaps Luther's most famous written work (and I
certainly believe his most important), was written
in response to *The Diatribe* of Erasmus. That is his
work on *The Bondage of the Will*. In *The Bondage of
the Will,* when Luther was responding to the attacks of Erasmus, he quoted Erasmus where
Erasmus said that on matters of difficult doctrines
like predestination, election, and issues of freedom
of the will and so on, he (Erasmus) preferred to
"suspend judgment," and that the proper academic
posture of the scholar, when investigating issues
like this, is to be very cautious, to reserve judgment,
and to hesitate from coming to firm conclusions.

Erasmus said that he would prefer not to make assertions. When Erasmus said to Luther, "I would prefer not to make assertions," Luther became apoplectic. He said, "You would prefer what? You don't want to make assertions? Take away assertions, and you take away Christianity. The very mark of the Christian is that the Christian boldly makes assertions before the world." Then, in his passion, Luther said, "The Holy Spirit is not a skeptic. And the things that He revealed are more certain than life itself. Away with the skeptics! Away with the academics!" Luther would have none of the spirit of those who are always learning and never coming to a knowledge of the truth. The early truth was built on the blood of the martyrs, and the reason why it was so bloody was because the apostles didn't go into the market place saying, "Well, maybe Jesus rose from the dead or maybe He didn't. You need to examine this, and suspend judgment." No, they were bold in their assertions because they knew that which they believed. They understood the things of God, were convinced of the truth of the claims of Jesus, and, having that assurance and certainty of the truthfulness and trustworthiness of Scripture, they went boldly into a dying world. Luther did the same.

Luther was certain about the doctrine of justification. Without the assurance he had that the Bible taught that doctrine, he could never have stood against the world, and against all the authority structures of his day. He wanted and expected the same kind of certainty from every minister—again, not a dogmatic spirit born out of arrogance, but that certainty that is rooted and grounded in a disciplined mastery of the Word of God. Both Luther and Calvin, even to this day, in the academic world, are regarded as being incredible geniuses who exhibited a rare and extraordinary mastery of their material. That is what ministers are called to do today, to master their material. The enterprise of preaching requires nothing less than that kind of due diligence. Why? Because their task is not to bark from the pulpit like barking dogs, woofing their opinions, but their task is to set forth with clarity and with boldness the Word of God.

A practicing psychologist from San Francisco came to me after a seminar on one occasion. She was very upset with her minister and opined, "I've come to the place where I am convinced that our minister is doing everything he possibly can to conceal the real nature of God from us in his preaching. He's so afraid that the preaching of the gospel might offend somebody, or that the setting forth of the character of God in His holiness, sovereignty, justice, and wrath will make people uncomfortable and cause them to leave the church.

I go to church to hear a word from God, and I'm starving to death in my church." I can't tell you how many telephone calls and how many letters I get from people all over America who basically echo those exact same sentiments. They're desperate; they're crying out to their pastors: "We're not interested in psychoanalysis on Sunday morning. We don't come to church to hear a commentary on the latest political issues in America. If we want that, we can turn on CNN or Fox Network, or we can go to the town meeting. We come to church to hear a word from God. We don't want your opinions. We want to hear a prophetic ministry that prefaces the sermon with the words, 'Thus saith the Lord.' "

This is how Luther and Calvin understood the task of the minister. The greatest awakening in the history of the church took place when, after the darkness had eclipsed the truth of the gospel and hidden the Word in obscurity, the light burst forth on the scene and awakened Christendom in the 16th century. That light was carried to churches by men who were bold enough to proclaim the Word of God and saw their task to be presenting the unembellished, undiluted, unvarnished Word of God. That is why they pored over the texts of Scripture, being careful of their exegesis before they entered the pulpit. Because that was the center of their task,

they were fearless. Their fearlessness, their boldness, their courage came from the conviction that
what they were preaching and teaching was the
Word of God.

It is interesting to me that we have a crisis in
the church in our day. We've seen a revolution in
worship which, in many ways, is being driven by
an attempt to be winsome to the people in our age.
As our society becomes more and more secular,
there is an attempt to rethink church, to remove all
of the artifacts of "churchiness": get rid of pulpits,
get rid of pews, turn the church building into what
looks like a concert hall, and turn worship into an
outreach ministry that comes across as exciting, interesting, and "entertaining." It's almost like we're
saying to our congregations today, "Let me entertain you." The number one hymn today may be,
"There's no business like show business."

The temptation to turn the pulpit into theater
and the church building into a place of entertainment is not something that just happened a few
decades ago. It was a problem that Luther struggled with in the 16th century. He said, when he
preached his most powerful sermons on justification by faith alone, that people fell asleep in his
congregation. He maintained that the people in the
parishes came to be entertained. Even in the 16th
century, the pastors, during the middle of the

Reformation, were struggling with the demands of their congregations that they entertain them with their preaching. Luther claimed that it is not the task of the pastor to entertain, but to nurture, to feed, and to be faithful to the Word of God. He said it is the task of the minister to protect the flock from heresy and from error. Today, if you preach against heresy and against error, you are entering into the arena of the politically incorrect because we live in a culture that has been captured by the spirit of relativism. Relativism says this: "truth is what you perceive it to be, and what is true for you may be false for somebody else."

In our present society, you're perfectly free to believe whatever you like, but the one thing you may not do is to deny its antithesis. You can say, "I believe that this is true." But you cannot say with impunity that that which opposes it is false. We have a whole generation of Christians who have been brainwashed by the spirit of relativism so they're completely hesitant to say, "I deny that error over there." We don't have heresy trials anymore because, in relativism, there is no such thing as heresy.

In discussions over the 2000 presidential election, when the Supreme Court was brought in to decide the matter, and oral hearings were presented before the bench of the Supreme Court,

Sandra Day O'Connor raised the question about voter responsibility. She commented that people have directions that tell them how to operate the voting machine, and that they are warned in the instructions to be sure that the stylus penetrates, and that there aren't any loose chads left hanging. This is the responsibility of the person who goes in to cast a vote.

One of the news commentators heard her comments, and declared that the assumption that Sandra Day O'Connor was making was that in America it is a privilege to vote, and with that privilege comes a corresponding responsibility. But he questioned, "Doesn't she understand that in our culture there is no such thing as responsibility." In a relativistic environment, you can't hold someone responsible for anything.

Even before relativism became fashionable, Luther had to deal with the responsibility of the good shepherd to protect his sheep from damage, from error, from false teachers. Luther understood that in Old Testament Israel, the greatest threat to the security of the nation was not the army of the Syrians, the Assyrians, the Babylonians, or the Philistines. What crushed Old Testament Israel was the false prophet within their gates. Jeremiah stood before God saying, "Lord, I quit. I will speak no more in your name. I am in derision daily."

Every time Jeremiah opened his mouth and proclaimed the Word of God to Jerusalem, there were
a hundred false prophets who would answer him
by telling the people, "Peace, peace," when there
was no peace. The people didn't want to hear the
bad news that Jeremiah was prophesying, and so
they heaped to themselves false teachers because
they had itching ears. They went to hear the teachers and the preachers who preached to them what
they wanted to hear.

Jeremiah complained about this. "God, these
people, these prophets, are dreaming up this stuff.
They heal the wound of the Daughter of Zion
slightly." When he complained to God he said,
"God, you have deceived me, and I am deceived.
You've overwhelmed me, and I am overwhelmed."
But what did God say to him? "Jeremiah, let the
prophet who has a dream tell his dream. As the
Psalmist says, 'Fret not yourselves over evildoers.' It
is not your concern. Let them tell their dream. I'll
take care of them. But let the man of God preach
the Word of God faithfully."

In the metaphor of the sheep, the false prophet
was the wolf in sheep's clothing. The false prophet
was the one who came in and preached in a religious setting to the sheep of the household of God.
What they were preaching was to the people's everlasting destruction and ruin. The true prophet or

the good shepherd lays down his life for his sheep. There is a reason why the good shepherd has that staff and the rod. They are to protect the sheep from the wolves who would come in and ravage them. Luther said that the false teacher, the false preacher, is the worst of all possible criminals, because he spreads a poison that has everlasting consequences and the pastor must protect his sheep from that criminal element.

Finally, Luther said that it is the task of the preacher to defend not the preacher's honor, but the honor of God and the honor of Christ. That is where the preacher rises to defend the truth—not to protect his own opinion or his own reputation, but to rise in defense of the honor of God and the honor of Jesus Christ. That is the duty of the pastor because the honor of God has been all but destroyed, not from outside the church in our day but from inside the church. I tell my seminary students, "Don't ever, ever, ever, ever preach your own anger. If you're angry about something, recuse yourself from preaching on that issue. Don't ever use the pulpit as your personal soapbox. If you want to proclaim the wrath of God, you'd better make sure it's God's wrath and not your own. You should be clear that your concern is the honor of Christ and not your own honor. Every minister brings his flesh with him into the pulpit. It is a sacred thing to guard against using the flesh and not the spirit of the Word of God."

For the Reformers, the center of worship was to be the hearing of the Word of God; and the center of that preaching, according to Luther, was to preach Christ. Luther approached this with an emphasis on the gospel, but not exclusively on the gospel. He made an important distinction to subsequent Lutheran theology (and to Reformation theology) between law and gospel. He was convinced that preachers ought to preach the law as well as the gospel because, unless the law is set forth clearly and unambiguously, people will never have an appreciation for the gospel. In one sense Luther anticipated where we are today, where the gospel has fallen almost into obscurity. People are not excited about the gospel because they tacitly assume that there is no great need for it. We are told that God loves everybody, and He loves them unconditionally; that He accepts us just as we are. If that were true, we would have no need to flee from our guilt and sin to embrace the gospel. Luther himself was almost completely crushed by his study of the law. As we look at his personal history in the monastery we see he spent hours every day in confession, repeating to his father confessor all his sins he could recall from the previous twenty-four hours. His confessor finally was frustrated, thinking that if he was going to confess sins, he ought to confess something big, not things such as "I coveted Brother David's morsel of meat on his plate last night," or "I stayed up five minutes past lights out reading my Bible by candlelight." What kind of trouble can you get into in a monastery that would take two or three hours to confess the next day?

But remember that Luther had been educated in jurisprudence. He was a promising student of law before he fled for refuge from the wrath of God into the monastery. So Luther would pore over the biblical law, and he saw the law as a mirror that revealed, on the one hand, the perfect righteousness and holiness of God. On the other hand, when Luther looked into that mirror, he saw the contrast between the righteousness of God and his own personal lack of righteousness. So if there ever was a person tormented by guilt and by the law of God, it was Luther. Luther said later that before God will allow people to experience the sweetness and joy of heaven, He first dangles them, as it were, over the pit of hell so that they can see what their estate would be apart from the gospel.

Luther on one occasion made his famous outburst: "You ask me if I love God? Love God? Sometimes I hate Him!" How could he say such a thing? Luther saw Christ as a stern and angry

Judge who was going to impose God's standard of righteousness upon him. Luther's thoughts would anticipate Agricola's sentiments when he said, "To the gallows with Moses!"

Luther also was captured by what Paul calls the pedagogical function of the law. Paul speaks of the law as the divine pedagogue—that is, the one who is the schoolmaster who brings us to Christ. That particular metaphor can be a little bit misleading to us. In the ancient world there were two adults in the classroom. One would communicate the information necessary for learning; he transferred the content. The other person carried a long stick and was basically the disciplinarian. If students in the classroom misbehaved or got out of line, the disciplinarian would come along and tap them on the shoulder lightly. If it became more severe, they would tap them not so gently the next time. That is what Paul was saying was the function of the law. The law is what corrects, disciplines, and exposes our evil, and therefore, drives us to the gospel.

One of the ancient issues that Augustine dealt with, with the heretic Pelagius, was whether God is unjust in commanding perfection from human beings. Augustine said that we are fallen and dead in sin and trespasses. Therefore we cannot fulfill the mandate that God gives to us to be holy even as He is holy. Pelagius countered that when God commands us to be holy and perfect, He could only do that if indeed we have the ability in and of ourselves to become perfect. Pelagius's heresy has been categorically rejected by the church on many occasions. However Luther struggled with this: Why would God, knowing that we can't fulfill some of the laws that He gives to his people, give them anyway? Luther called that the evangelical function of the law.

The evangelical function of the law is to drive us to the gospel. In the church I pastor, we read from the Ten Commandments each Sunday morning, with a brief exposition of one of them. We do this for the same reason Luther and Calvin agreed upon in the 16th century. We must keep the law of God before the people so that they may lay hold of the gospel. Luther's great fear in his older years was that the gospel that had been recovered during the Reformation would go once again into obscurity. He said that every time the gospel is preached with clarity and with boldness, it produces conflict. He knew that people flee from conflict, and he feared that they would stop preaching the gospel with clarity and with boldness in order to avoid conflict. He predicted what we are experiencing now, and the light of the gospel is growing dim.

Luther saw that the task of the preacher is to constantly preach law and gospel, but if you are going to err in one direction it is better to err on the side of the gospel than on the side of the law. Never would he allow the possibility of merely preaching the gospel without ever preaching the law. If all you preach is the "good news," and you never preach the "bad news," the "good news" becomes "no news," and it is not significant to people.

Luther also said that the minister should never be engaged in preaching novelties. That is an interesting insight; because in the theological world we often put a premium on the value of coming up with something new and different. Of course Luther offered brilliant insights, vignettes of discernment into the Word of God that in many ways were exceedingly fresh and helpful in awakening the people of his day. It's one thing for a minister to communicate a vignette of insight drawn from the text itself, that we may have forgotten or overlooked, but Luther was talking about creative invention. There is no room for that in the pulpit, and there is no room for that in the teaching of the people of God.

One of the problems we have in the church today is the theological crisis of liberal theology that has captured many of the mainline denominations where the ministers no longer teach from the content of Scripture at all. How does that happen historically? It is axiomatic that as the seminaries go, so go the pastors; and as the pastors go, so go the congregations. If you want a reformation, you have to look seriously at what the seminaries are teaching.

Seminaries are academic institutions, and they are always competing for academic respectability. They want the professors with the best credentials from the most acclaimed universities. At the academic level, in order to get a doctor's degree, you have to publish a doctoral dissertation. In most institutions, in order to qualify for a Ph.D. dissertation, you have to come up with a thesis that is new. So we put a premium on novelty. It is one thing for somebody engaged in chemical research to discover new insights in terms of how certain chemicals interact with each other. The sciences, particularly the physical sciences, are subjected to great advances with further research and novel experimentation. When we talk about understanding the content of a book that was completed 2,000 years ago, with the best minds in Western history having pored over the content of the texts, it is highly unlikely that we will come up with a radical, new insight that will change the whole dimension of understanding that book. Yet we put pressure on our scholars to do just that.

When I was in graduate school, I read about a student at the University of Manchester in England

who received his Ph.D. for a thesis that claimed
that there was a particular mushroom that was a
hallucinogenic and incited people to all kinds of
sexual eroticism, and Jesus founded a cult based
upon that. That kind of thing is manifestly absurd.
One has to completely ignore all of the classical
standards of historical research to come up with
such a thesis. But in our day, the more novel something is, the more enticing it becomes for academic
recognition.

On a television show recently I was asked about
the Jesus Seminar, and I said that there is a left
and a right wing in theological scholarship. Not
only that, there is also a radical right and a radical
left. In addition to the radical right, there is also
have what we call the lunatic fringe. The lunatic
fringe on the left wing is called "the Jesus
Seminar." People ask if I am serious with my
comment because the Jesus Seminar people are
scholars. I reply that, though these people went to
school and got degrees, they represent the lunatic
fringe of academic investigation to historical reality.
That is, they are utterly irresponsible, and they do
not practice sober scholarship. I can find myself on
the completely opposite end of the spectrum from
some higher critical liberal scholar, and yet at the
same time respect his methodology, his manner of
academic research. However, the Jesus Seminar is

what I call the sensational phase. That is, it attracts the press because it is novel. Remember when Paul gathered with the philosophers at the Areopagus, it was said of those philosophers who gathered there for discussion daily that they were always there to discuss what was new; that's the only reason they gave Paul a hearing, because he was coming up with a novelty, that someone had actually been raised from the dead.

What God expects from a minister of the gospel is the sober, accurate presentation of His Word. We get no style points for novelty from God. In fact, to be novel with the Word of God is to create something that is not a part of the Word of God, and is to add to the Word what does not belong to it. At that point we place ourselves before the wrath of God. According to Luther, there is no room for novelty; we are to preach the whole counsel of God, the law in its fullness, the gospel in its fullness, with no inventions.

It is our task to show people how to get to heaven. Some people look at that and smile from the 20th-century perspective. "Are you serious, Luther, that the task of the preacher on Sunday morning is to teach people how to get to heaven? Isn't that so 'other worldly' in its orientation that we lose the application of the Word of God to the present?" they would inquire.

Luther said that the task of the church is profane. The entymological derivation of profane literally means "out of the temple," or "outside of the temple." Luther said that the Christian life is to be so strong that we go out of the temple and into the world. By learning how to get to heaven on the vertical plane, we also learn how to be Christ for our neighbor on the horizontal plane, so that, after we come out of church on Sunday morning, we go into the world with the gospel. He does not mean that we are to be profane people in the negative sense of that word, as it is used in our language today. Luther did not see the task of the church to be contained in a monastery someplace, but that the Word of God penetrate the culture and the strongholds of this world.

That is a far cry from what happened in the 19th century, where the liberal theology completely denied the importance and value of the vertical relationship. They said Christianity is not about how to get to heaven; it is how to love our neighbor. It is not about supernatural reconciliation, but rather it is about building a humanitarian society. So the gospel became translated into the so-called "social gospel" of the 19th century.

Luther claimed that every person's most acute need during their life is what happens to them at the end of that life when they die. The Word of

God and the preacher of the Word of God are to prepare every person for making that transition from this world into heaven. As pastors we are entrusted with the souls of people and their eternal destiny. We live in a day when people don't even believe that we have souls; but essential to the Christian faith is the doctrine of the personal continuity of our existence after our death. We need to be prepared for that, and that is the task of the preacher.

One of the reasons ministers try to conjure up new and interesting viewpoints is because there is a lack of confidence among preachers in the effectiveness of preaching the whole counsel of God. Luther strongly emphasized that the power of preaching resides not in the preacher or in the method or in the technique, but the power of preaching is found in the power of God who attends the proclamation of His Word. Of course Luther understood, with respect to the gospel, that the gospel in the first instance does not belong to the preacher. It doesn't even belong to the church. Paul articulates in the first chapter of Romans that he is an apostle separated by God to the gospel of God. He uses the expression, "the gospel of God." This "of" does not mean "about," rather it is the possessive form. And when Paul speaks of the gospel of God, what he is saying is that the gospel belongs to God. He is its Author; He is its Owner. The gospel is not something invented by the insights of prophets or preachers, but the gospel comes from God Himself. He owns it. It is His property. So when we are proclaiming the gospel, we are proclaiming a message that is not our own.

Later in that same epistle Paul says that the gospel is the power of God unto salvation for all who believe—that the power is in the gospel, not in our presentation of it. That being the case, it is all the more necessary for the preacher to be careful in how he sets forth the gospel.

A few years ago at a Christian bookseller's convention, with several thousand people present, one Christian group did a survey asking people to define the gospel. A hundred people responded. Those who sponsored the survey looked at the responses, and only one out of a hundred qualified as an adequate description of the gospel. People think that the gospel is having a warm relationship with Jesus, or asking Christ into your heart. Those things are important, but that is not the gospel. The gospel has a clear content that focuses on the person of Christ, the work of Christ, and how the benefits of Christ are appropriated into the Christian's life by faith.

Our first task as preachers is to make sure we know the gospel ourselves, so that we can then proclaim it accurately and boldly. When we do that, it is not our responsibility to make sure that the gospel takes hold in the hearts of men, or that the gospel produces a response of faith. Paul wrote to the Ephesians that we are justified by grace through faith, and that is not of ourselves; it is the gift of God. Even the faith that we hope will be the response to the proclaiming of the gospel is not something that we can create; but it is a gift from God. So I can preach with the greatest eloquence, the greatest sincerity, with the most modern techniques possible, to multitudes of people, and not see any fruit. Or I can, with very little talent, set forth the minimal content of the gospel and see a revival break out, because the power is in the gospel as God attends the preaching of His Word. Remember that God has chosen the foolishness of preaching as the means by which He will save the world.

The Bible puts a premium on the office of preaching. He has chosen the foolishness of preaching as the means for His end to bring salvation to bear in the people. Luther understood that when he said, "Your task, O preacher, is to make sure that you are faithful to the text, that you are faithful to the proclamation of that gospel, that you are faithful to set forth the whole counsel of God, and then step back and let it happen. I don't have

to try to cajole and persuade people with my techniques to get them to respond. I preach the law; I
preach the gospel, and it is the Holy Ghost who attends the ministry of that word to bring forth the
fruit."

Luther explains that God has entrusted the ministry of the Word to us, not its results, just as He
did in the days of Moses, when God sent Moses to
Pharaoh. If ever there was a power struggle set
forth in Scripture, it was the struggle with Moses
and Pharaoh, who was the most powerful man in
the world at the time. God sent Moses, an exile,
who had been living for years as a shepherd in the
Midianite wilderness, to go to Pharaoh and to
command him in the name of God to let His people go. Against the forces of this world, Moses was
impotent. He had nothing in himself to compare
with the power of Pharaoh. Moses was faithful, and
God tore down the mighty from their thrones, and
vanquished all of the power that Pharaoh could
bring to bear on the situation.

For this reason, Luther had a high degree of respect for ministers who were faithful to the Word.
He said that the people of God should give high
honor and esteem to their preachers, and especially
to mediocre preachers. It is interesting that we live
in an economy where the value of goods and services are determined by the marketplace. I can't tell

you how valuable your car is to you; only you know its value to you. But in our culture we tend to put a high price on automobiles because we're a highly mobilized society, and we frequently live many miles from our workplace. We need transportation, so we're willing to spend large amounts in order to have a car. We put a premium on our physical health, and so we're willing to spend large amounts of money for doctors and medical care.

But watch the cultural habits of people when they go to church. Thirty years ago, the custom was to drop a one dollar bill into the collection basket as it was passed. Today the custom is to put a one dollar bill in the basket—never mind inflation. If we leave it up to the marketplace, we will see that the lowest paid professionals in America are teachers and preachers. Why is that? Because we don't place much value upon the services they provide. That is why, in Old Testament Israel, God commanded a tax upon the people of Israel, the tithe. It was distributed among the Levites who were responsible for teaching and for preaching. God knew that if the value of preaching were left to people, they would never pay for it. Luther said that is a sin against God that we have such a low view and low value of preachers.

At this point the culture will come back and say, "We want our preachers to be poor because we don't want them to be worldly." It is never our responsibility to take care of other people's charity; you're responsible for your own charity, not to impose it upon other people. When Luther saw this going on in Germany, he said, "Even the mediocre preacher is bringing the pearl of great price to the people; that which is of eternal, inestimable value is being handled by the minister, and we ought not to despise the labor that is brought forth by those."

On the other hand, he said the thing that is often the snare to the faithful preacher is personal ambition. You may think that somewhat strange because you may question why a man would go into the ministry out of personal ambition. One of the attractive things about the ministry is that it gives a person an instant place of leadership, speaking, and of influencing other people. Even if the pay isn't much, the authority level or the power of the pulpit can still be an enticement to people who have no regard for the things of God. Luther cautioned men to be careful of the ambition that can destroy the ministry. He said that the people most vulnerable to that destruction in ministry are the ones who are most talented, because the most talented preachers and teachers are the ones most vulnerable to pride. It is pride that becomes the snare to the minister who now has something to lose, and he begins to build his own empire rather than being faithful to the things of God.

We do not put our trust in technique. Nevertheless Luther did not despise the teaching of certain principles of communication that he thought were important. There are things that preachers can learn regarding how to construct and deliver a sermon, and how to communicate information effectively from the pulpit. He also said that the structure of the human person is an important clue to preaching. God has made us in His image and He has given to us minds. The word was meant to be understood.

The sermon is addressed to the mind, but it's not just a communication of information—there is also admonition and exhortation. There is a sense in which we are addressing people's will and are calling them to move. We call them to act according to their understanding. In other words, we want to get to the heart; but we know that the way to the heart is through the mind. So, first of all, the people must be able to understand what we're talking about. That is why Luther says it is one thing to be teaching in seminary, as he was at the university, but on Sunday morning, he said, "I preach to little Hans and to little Elizabeth. I pitch my sermons to the children of the congregation to make sure that everybody in the room can understand. The sermon is not an exercise in abstract thinking." Therefore, that which makes the deepest and most long-lasting impression on people is concrete illustrations. For Luther, the three most important principles of public communication are illustrate, illustrate, illustrate. That is why he encouraged the preacher to use concrete images and narratives. He advises that, when preaching on abstract doctrine, the pastor find a narrative in Scripture that communicates that truth, and to communicate the abstract through the concrete.

That is how Jesus preached. Somebody came to Him and wanted to debate what it means to love your neighbor as much as you love yourself. The lawyer said to Jesus, "Who is my neighbor?" Jesus replied, "A man went down from Jericho and fell among thieves. . . ." He told the story of the Good Samaritan. He didn't just give an abstract, theoretical answer to the question, who is my neighbor? He answered it in the concrete by giving a real-life situation to illustrate what He was talking about.

Jonathan Edwards preached his famous "Sinners in the Hands of an Angry God" sermon in Enfield, Connecticut. He preached that sermon reading it in a monotone from a draft of the sermon, and said, "O sinner, you are hanging, as it were, over the pit of hell, much as a spider hangs by a single thread over a flame." Edwards used these images taken largely from the Bible: "God's bow is bent, and the arrow of His wrath is aimed at your heart. You are like people walking across a canyon on a slippery bridge where the planks on the bridge are rotted and your feet will slide and slip at any moment and plunge you into the abyss." What Edwards understood was, the more graphic the image, the more people were likely to hear it and to remember it. Luther said the same thing. However, at this point he is not substituting technique for substance, but saying that the substance of the Word of God must be communicated in simple, graphic, straightforward, illustrative ways to the people of God. And in this the Word of God is communicated. That is the whole of the matter for Luther, that the function of the minister is to be a carrier, a bearer of the Word of God—nothing less, nothing more.

Preaching to the Mind

John Armstrong

In 2 Timothy 4, the Apostle Paul exhorts Timothy to preach the Word with careful instruction, because the time will come when men will not put up with sound doctrine.

> In the presence of God and of Christ Jesus, who will judge the living and the dead, and in view of His appearing and His kingdom, I give you this charge. Preach the Word. Be prepared in season and out of season. Correct, rebuke and encourage, with great patience and careful instruction. For the time will come when men will not put up with sound doctrine. Instead, to suit their own desires, they will gather around them a great number of teachers to say what their itching ears want to hear. They will turn their ears away from the truth, and turn aside to myths. But you, keep your head in all situations; endure hardship; do the work of an evangelist; discharge all the duties of your ministry. For I am already being poured out like a drink offering, and the time has come for my departure. I have fought the good fight; I have finished the race; I have kept the faith. Now there is in store for me the crown of righ-

teousness which the Lord, the righteous
Judge, will award to me on that day—and not
only to me, but also to all who have longed for
His appearing.

These verses from Romans chapter 12 are also
familiar.

Therefore, I urge you brothers, in view of
God's mercy, to offer your bodies as living
sacrifices, holy and pleasing to God—this is
your spiritual act of worship. Do not conform
any longer to the pattern of this world, but be
transformed by the renewing of your mind.

Be transformed by the renewing of your mind.
How do we preach for the renewing of the mind?
What is the preaching that aims intentionally at
impacting and changing, at instructing with all
long-suffering patience, the mind? There have been
times in our history when it would have been almost oxymoronic to talk about preaching to the
mind. The time in which we now live is not such a
time. Our culture is an amusement culture. I have
at times pondered the word "amusement." "Muse"
means "to think." The "ment" at the end of the
word means "to be in the state of." And to put an
"a" in front of it makes the word mean "to be in a
state of non-thinking." That's really where our culture is. We have book titles like *The Dumbing Down*

of America, or *The Closing of the American Mind,* or
Amusing Ourselves to Death, probably the best of
such titles written by the critic Neal Postman.
Postman makes the case that we live in an
amusement-based culture, a culture that is primarily interested in entertainment. The great tragedy is
that now we are being told the way to market the
church, the way to build the church, the way to
grow the church, is to play our cards, as it were, in
the direction of such a culture; to not only understand it, but to pitch our message, our ministry, our
preaching, if we dare call some of this preaching,
in the direction of amusement. Think of it! We are
called to the ministry of apostolic amusement.
Certainly that is oxymoronic, if there was ever was
such: *apostolic amusement.* These apostles did anything but amuse their hearers. Disturb, yes.
Trouble, yes. But amuse? Never!

Truth renews the mind. Indeed, the truth which
would affect the heart, which moves the heart,
which changes the heart, must first enter through
the vestibule of the mind if it would enter the sanctuary of the heart. The intention of truth preached
is to affect the emotions and the will and the heart
and the whole of our humanity. Truth, as Phillips
Brooks once said, is preaching which passes
through our humanity to the humanity of those
who hear us, and thus preaching must come first

through the mind. It makes its appeal through the mind; it enters through the mind—but it doesn't simply stop with the mind if it is biblical preaching. We must understand that it starts here.

Truth is an inevitable expression of our concern with God—God who is the measure of all things, who reveals to us His mind. He reveals His mind to us in the words of sacred Scripture so that we might hear and understand the mind of God. Therefore, not to be driven by the question "What is truth?" is to fail to understand and to be properly God-centered. Thus all preaching that reaches the mind must be theological preaching. Yes, we must unabashedly, unashamedly say that preaching must be theological preaching. Not theology as an end in itself, but as an expression of our attempts to understand God's mind, to understand the revelation of God. His truth comes to our minds and moves our hearts to worship and to adore. "Oh, come, let us adore Him, let us adore Him, Christ the Lord." How do we adore Him? Through the truth reaching our minds. Every Christian then is a theologian. As the late Dr. John Gerstner used to say, every Christian is a theologian—a good one, a bad one or an indifferent one, but every Christian is a theologian. All Christians must be taught to think and to have their minds renewed, so that they are not conformed to the pattern of this world, but are transformed by the renewing of their mind.

But what does theology have to do with this, especially in a time when the Queen of Sciences is anything but a queen or a king in the affections of those who are professed followers of Christ? There is a vast difference between understanding the truth at the level of intellectually affirming a creed, and understanding the value and the place of God-centeredness in theology. We must understand what theology is. Our people must understand what theology is, that it is the study of God. It is the inquiry of God. It is the searching and understanding of God and the meaning of His word, His truth and His revelation. It is the activity of thinking: thinking about God and asking ultimate questions. It is the activity that thought produces speech, and speech produces a reflection we might call "theologizing," or "doing theology," as it is sometimes called.

We may also speak of theology as the product of that activity which seeks to inquire and to understand. Sometimes in historical theology we speak of "Luther's theology," or "Calvin's theology," or "Puritan theology." Now we must understand that the chief opponents of our Lord Jesus Christ were theologians. At the same time we must understand that those who followed our Lord carefully were also theologians.

Some time ago I was part of a discussion where a prominent Christian leader, at the end of a two-hour discussion about the church, doctrine, theology, and salvation, was asked to stand up and lead us in closing prayer. I'll never forget his closing words: "Before I pray I have one statement to make. I'm so glad that I met Jesus before I ever met a theologian." I think he spoke for a great number of evangelical people when he made that statement after a discussion of theological implications, inferences, and issues. We have divorced theology and the mind. We have also divorced understanding from the heart and from the affections and the will. But the biblical pattern is to move people to do what is right by moving them to think what is right, to understand what is right. This is the work of theology. To reject theology is to reject the knowledge of God, which is never an option for believers.

The temper of our modern mind has reversed the priority and has placed the mind in a sort of secondary position. What is primary now are the actions, the will, and the response. Yet I remind you that it was our Lord who said that the first and great commandment (Matthew 22:37) is that we are to love the Lord our God with all our heart, with all our soul, and with *all our mind*. If we would love God with our heart, if we would love God with our soul, we must love God with our mind. We must learn to embrace the sacred mysteries, but we must do so by grappling and wrestling with our minds, seeking to get our minds around truth that will expand our thoughts, that will humble us before the magnitude of such truth. We must learn further to resist the pressures that our culture brings upon our minds to be evasive, to be imprecise.

This is one of the great problems of our day. If you converse with people regarding Christian doctrine, you'll find that this evasiveness is very common. Imprecision, the loss of language, is thus another concern. J. Gresham Machen understood this when he wrote his classic *What Is Faith?* He said this temper of mind, this temper to be imprecise and evasive of saying anything specific is hostile to *precise* definitions. "Indeed," said Machen, "nothing makes a man more unpopular in the controversies of the present day than an insistence upon definitions of terms. Men discourse eloquently today upon such subjects as God, religion, Christianity, atonement, redemption, and faith, but they are greatly incensed when they are asked to tell in simple language what they mean by these terms. You speak of Christ? What Christ? You speak of atonement? What atonement? What is the nature of the atonement? Faith? What kind of faith? What is the nature of the faith that you speak of?"

We must teach the mind biblical truth in such a way that people understand what we are really saying. The older evangelicalism was driven by a passion for truth, thus it had a passion to be more precise. This is why it could express itself not in sociological language, nor in psychological language, but in theological terms. This is why older evangelicalism insisted upon a clear theological vocabulary. This is why they didn't have discussions about communicating without theological words. They sought to define words, to explain words, to illustrate words, but they would have never thought of communicating without using precise words, as we do today. David Wells captured this when he wrote, "The new evangelicalism is not driven by the same passion for truth as the older form, and that is why it is often empty of theological interest. We now have less biblical fidelity, less interest in the truth, less seriousness, less depth and less capacity to speak the Word of God to our own generation in a way that offers an alternative to what it already thinks."

Today, instead of using language and being precise in definition in our preaching, we are being summoned by the siren calls of seminaries, denominations, workshops, and seminars to do something quite different, and that is to pitch our message in the direction of the culture and "felt needs,"

whatever those are. The last I examined "felt
needs," it came from a man called Abraham
Maslow, not from Paul or Peter. When we begin to
pitch our message in the direction of so-called "felt
needs," we baptize this thinking. When you do
that, you have a radical distinction from what the
church has known and has contended for apolo-
getically through the centuries. Words have meaning, and thus consequences. And words like
"atonement," "faith," and "repentance" have meaning and consequence. We say, "Well, we must
speak to people." Yes, we must speak to people; we
must speak to them as the servants of Christ, and
our *manner* is as important as our *matter*. But we
must have matter even if we have proper manner. It
is not simply impressing ourselves upon people.
One of the most popularized spokespersons of the
church growth movement over the last three to four
decades is Lyle Schaller. His great concern has
been for the mainline churches and their shrinking
population. A few years ago he was interviewed in
the *Chicago Tribune,* and he made an astounding
statement (I think his observation is right). He
said, "For the church what matters is not the message; what matters today is the man." What matters is not the message, but the man. Now both
matter, obviously. But see how the whole process
has been turned upside down. Schaller is actually

only reflecting what really is the case in most churches. What matters is the man. What matters is the stuff that the man brings to the occasion, not the substance or the weight of his message.

We need to be very forthright about all this. Ultimately, it is a case of untruth in distinction from truth. Where does untruth come from? Paul says very clearly in 2 Corinthians 4 that untruth is that which comes from the evil one. Therefore it is imperative that we seek to explain the truth to our people, that we preach the truth, that we show them the truth, that we not only live the truth (which we must as ministers of the gospel), but we must preach the truth. We must love the truth. We must buy the truth, as Scripture says, and sell it not. How do we do this? Let me suggest several ways:

1. We must show repeatedly, by both our manner and our matter, that God is truth. When our Lord says, "I am the Way, the Truth, and the Life; no one comes to the Father but by Me," He is saying that God is truth. We must show our hearers repeatedly that God is truth.

2. We need to show our hearers regularly that failure to love the truth invites spiritual destruction. In 2 Thessalonians 2:8ff, Paul makes it very clear that if you do not love the truth, embrace the truth, and hold to the truth, you will be destroyed; you

will perish. Our hearers must understand; our congregation must feel the weight of our concern for truth in such a way that they know that we believe this whether they believe it or not. To not love and embrace the truth, to not worship God in Spirit and in truth, invites spiritual destruction. It is not a matter of "a better way," or "the best way," it is a matter of the only way. If you would know God, you must know him "in truth" and you must worship Him "in truth." Measure what you do by truth, because truth matters.

3. Truth is necessary for salvation. There is no salvation without the truth. Vast numbers of members of conservative churches do not understand this today. Listen to the Apostle Paul in 2 Thessalonians 2:13: "But we ought always to thank God for you, brothers loved by the Lord, because from the beginning God chose you to be saved through the sanctifying work of the Spirit and through belief in the truth." God chose you; God elected you on the basis of Christ and grace to be saved, to be delivered, to be redeemed through the sanctifying work of the Spirit and belief in the truth. Without the truth there is no salvation. We must impress this upon our hearers regularly.

4. Truth, and this I find very convincing in the face of modern psychologizing, was more important to the early church's ministry than motives.

Think back to Philippians 1 and Paul's moment of autobiographical insight into what had happened to him with the Philippian believers. He was more concerned that Christ be preached than whether or not Paul be recognized or Paul appreciated. Whether or not the motives of those who preached were good or bad, Paul rejoiced if Christ was preached. By simple deduction and observation, truth was of more importance to the apostle and to the apostolic church than motives. That is not to say motives are unimportant; God searches the heart and judges the motives. But truth was the priority. In Galatians 1:6–9 Paul says that the gospel is measurable. It's as if you can take a person to a wall and draw a line and say "Here is a six foot mark, and you're five feet, ten and three-quarter inches; you fall short of the mark." There is an objective standard by which we can measure. It is called the truth; it is called the gospel.

5. Preaching the truth is the apostolic method for church planting. This can be observed again and again in the book of Acts. Acts 17:2: "As his *custom* was, Paul went into the synagogue. And on three Sabbath days he reasoned with them from the Scriptures." Here's a great pattern for building a church. Paul went to a place where he found religious people, some interest in God and the worship of God and concern with ultimate truth, and

he reasoned with them from the Scriptures. Verse 3: "...explaining and proving"—explaining from the Scriptures and proving, obviously from the Old Testament Scriptures, no less—"that the Christ, the Messiah, had to suffer and rise from the dead."

Have you ever asked how He did that? You ought to. Could you or I prove that the Messiah had to die, suffer, and rise from the dead with the Scriptures of the Old Testament? If you're going to preach Christ from the whole of the Bible, which you ought to do, then you need to wrestle with that question. You do this by proving and explaining that "Christ had to suffer and rise from the dead, [that] this Jesus I'm proclaiming to you is the Christ; the Jesus of Nazareth that I'm speaking of, that I'm preaching to you, is the Messiah." This text adds that, "some of the Jews were persuaded and joined Paul and Silas, as did a large number of God-fearing Greeks, and not a few prominent women." There was a church growth movement; it was the result of opening the Scriptures, of explaining and convincing with the Scriptures that Jesus is the Christ.

In Acts 18, we are told that every Sabbath Paul reasoned in the synagogue, trying to persuade Jews and Greeks. When Silas and Timothy came from Macedonia, Paul devoted himself exclusively to preaching, to testifying to the Jews that Jesus was the Christ. But when the Jews opposed Paul and became abusive, he shook out his clothes in protest and said to them, "Your blood be on your own heads. I am clear of my responsibility; from now on I will go to the Gentiles." Then Paul left the synagogue. He went next door to the house of Titius Justus, a worshiper of God. Crispus the synagogue ruler and his entire household believed in the Lord, and many of the Corinthians who heard him believed and were baptized. The Lord, of course, comes and gives Paul the vision about not being silent but continuing to preach in the midst of some fears he had. Verse 11: "So Paul stayed for a year and a half, teaching them the Word of God." A year and a half, teaching, teaching, teaching—line upon line, precept upon precept—the Word of God. The method of the apostle was the Word! The method he used was persuading: logical, careful, thoughtful persuasion, demonstrating that the Scriptures pointed to Jesus of Nazareth, that He would suffer as Messiah, that He would rise from the dead as Messiah on the third day, and that this was in fulfillment of what the Scriptures prophesied to the Jews.

But when he turned to the Greeks he didn't change his method; he preached Christ and Him crucified, Christ and Him raised from the dead. In Acts 19 we read that Paul entered the synagogue and spoke boldly there for three months, and here we encounter a word that wouldn't fit into most of our vocabularies today: "arguing persuasively about the kingdom of God." He was reasoning by means of argumentation, using rhetoric as the servant of his logical arguments that Jesus Christ was the King and the Sovereign, who came to establish the kingdom of God among those who would receive Him. He argued regarding the kingdom of God. But some of them became obstinate. "They refused to believe and publicly maligned The Way." So Paul left them. He took the disciples with them and had discussions daily in the lecture hall at Tyrannus. Apparently when he is thrown out of this public place, he just moves and rents a lecture hall and says, "I'll just keep on teaching and lec- turing and arguing and persuading." Verse 10: "This went on for two years, so that all the Jews and Greeks who lived in the province of Asia heard the Word of the Lord." What an amazing state- ment! What a church-planting methodology! It has not been tried and found wanting in our day; it has not even been seriously tried! This is not the way we plant churches; this is not the way we establish disciples today. This is not the hue and cry of modern evangelicalism, and yet it is a part of our historical tradition.

You find in the Great Awakenings that they of-

ten came when the church was at its lowest ebb
and very few people worshipped. The congregations were empty and the churches were dying. In
the providence of God, He thrust workers into the
harvest. He literally throws them out into the harvest fields, and the harvest fields are not the people
necessarily sitting in the pews (though sometimes
that is the case), but He throws them out into the
highways and the hedges. In former days, men traversed the lanes of Wales, preaching on tomb-
stones and doing radical things that shocked people. Ministers of the gospel like George Whitefield
preached with great imaginative skill and ability.
These were all very much individuals, but individuals anointed by God to go out to people to speak
persuasively and powerfully to their minds, to appeal to them to repent and to believe the gospel.

6. Christian living, biblically, is always based
and grounded upon obedience to the truth.
Christian living is always the working out of the
mind and its response in the life on the basis of
obedience to the truth. This is self-evident from
Romans 6:1–3; Romans 6:15–16; James 4:4. If you
take a concordance and look at the use of "truth,"
"mind," "obedience," and "response" throughout
Scripture, Christian living is grounded in obedience to the truth. When the apostles appealed to
persons to live up to what they were, as in Romans

6, Paul appealed to them to live in the light of the truth they confessed to have believed, to obey that truth. Indeed, in Romans that becomes a synonym for faith: *obedience to the truth*, the obedience of faith.

7. Christ's body must be built up. It must be built up in love, but how is it built up in love? The answer is by using the truth (Ephesians 4:11–15). The truth is used not as a means in itself, but to build up the body in love. We must understand that knowledge puffs up. That is a principle; it is a fact; it is a truism. But because knowledge puffs up, this does not mean we should forego the truth in order to minister, but rather we should maximize truth in love.

8. Apostolic ministry is a truth-driven ministry. This is demonstrated in 2 Corinthians 4:2 as well as 6:6. The church is described in 1 Timothy 3:15 as the pillar and foundation of the truth. The church is the expression of the truth. It is the living, viable, visible expression, the pillar and support system and the foundation of the truth in the world. Elders are to teach the truth and to present their hearers as complete in Christ by the truth. Elders must guard the truth. The ministry is a truth profession, as well as a character profession. Thus Jonathan Edwards properly reasoned that truth is the consistency and agreement of our ideas

with the ideas of God.

The question we need to ask ourselves is this: Are we passionate about the truth? Do our hearers believe that the truth matters to us, that it matters so much that we would lay down our lives for the truth? We must make truth the pursuit of our lives. The goal of our ministry is to get truth into our hearers, not just by pouring our own ideas into people, but by pouring the Word of God into our hearers. Our culture militates severely against this understanding of the mind and of truth, and of preaching and teaching in this way.

Perhaps the foremost leader of evangelical thinking about statistics and the impact of growth, among evangelicals in America, is the sociologist George Barna. He seems at times to influence the pulpit more than Peter, Paul, Edwards, Calvin, Luther or anyone else, at least in our modern scene. His book, *Marketing the Church*, actually takes the position that preachers are to preach in order to reach certain segments of our society. His basic thesis is that marketing the church continues as the dominant impact and direction of our preaching. In an article in the magazine *Preaching,* entitled "The Pulpit-meister Preaching to the New Majority," George Barna (who is not a preacher, who is not a theologian, but is a sociologist and a market strategist) departs from his usual role as sociologist and assumes the role of a professor. He states, "The core of our message must never be compromised." That, by the way, is repeatedly said in such literature, and that causes unwary consumer preachers to think everything is well in Zion because they have already been told that the core of the message must not be compromised. However, in this same article, Barna clearly proposes that what we do affects what we say. He suggests that the new majority, the group of so-called "boomers and busters," have certain characteristics which prevent them from being attentive to typical, traditional preaching—that means, preaching that is particularly aimed at the mind through the inculcation of truth by way of biblical doctrine and biblical language.

I recognize that preachers must develop their own style. I also recognize that preaching in certain parts of the world changes because of cultural influences. But when the preacher must change his language or excise it of theological and biblical content, he finds himself positioned to be more of an inspirational speaker and a motivator than a preacher of God's truth. We're told that our sermons must be under 20 minutes, filled with stories, avoiding moral absolutes, light on scriptural references. We have no hope in such a context of really teaching doctrine, adds Barna.

Interestingly, and not surprisingly, Barna's research in the last five years has noted that evangelicalism is slipping drastically, that its numbers are on the decline, and that the knowledge of basic Christian doctrines is precariously slipping in our evangelical churches. Forty nine percent of evangelicals don't believe that Jesus is God and man, or without sin. Between seventy and eighty percent say that, in the matter of salvation, God helps those who help themselves, which is historic Pelagianism. Barna indeed shows us the problem. But his solution is to avoid the absolutes, to go light on Scripture, not to explain the doctrines of the Word, but rather to be "practical." He goes so far as to state in this same article, "Increasingly we find that the entire approach of talking at the audience is an ill-fated form of communication." That is shorthand for, "Don't stand and talk for forty minutes to a group of people; they won't listen to you."

I admit that we live in a time when it is extremely difficult to talk for very long to people and keep their attention—not impossible, but difficult. Barna suggests that preaching, in any series of messages, will not work since the audience changes from week to week. So much for biblical exposition in a continuous fashion. The question that Barna's article raises is simply this: what are we trying to do in our preaching? What are we trying to accomplish? Are we trying to minister to the self-centeredness of people or proclaim "Thus saith the Lord"?

We must grapple with the biblical issue of preaching to the mind in such a way that we understand that we're not preaching simply to the emotions; we're not simply preaching sermons that are long on practical life application. This generally means that our sermons are especially sprinkled with references to the family, to money, and to politics. But we are preaching to the souls of our hearers by speaking to their minds from Scripture.

In his book *Preaching and Preachers*, D. Martyn Lloyd-Jones writes: "The most urgent need in the Christian church today is true preaching." And as the greatest and most urgent need in the church, it is obviously the greatest need of the world also. Do you believe the greatest need of the church today is true preaching because it is the Word of God?

What is preaching? Lloyd-Jones' answer to what is preaching is classic: "Preaching is logic on fire." It is reasoning with the mind by the Scripture that is set on fire by the Spirit of God. It is not entertaining the troops; it is not lecturing; it is not, as a friend of mine says about some preaching, "a data dump," backing the truck up and dumping the newest knowledge on your hearers. It is logic on fire. Lloyd-Jones goes on to add these words about preaching: "eloquent reason." Logic on fire and eloquent reason.

Most of us don't think of ourselves as eloquent, especially when we've heard eloquent preachers. I've known some eloquent preachers who were not great lovers of Christ, but had great gifts of eloquence. It is not that we should disdain eloquence; we should desire to be more eloquent; elocution is our task. Speaking plainly and clearly to the conscience of our hearers is our calling. We must reason with eloquence, but it must be logic on fire. Are these contradictions? Of course not. Reason concerning this truth ought to be mightily eloquent. As you see in the case of the Apostle Paul and others, it is theology on fire. Preaching is theology on fire. It is not theology in the classic textbook sense of headings and categories; you can kill a congregation with that approach. It is not even preaching through various systematic categories. But it is theology; it is reasoning God's thoughts from God's Word in such a way with the best eloquence we can bring to the task. By the power of the Spirit we speak of the theology that burns within us.

Says Lloyd-Jones finally, "And a theology which does not take fire, I maintain, is a defective theology, or at least the man's understanding of it is defective. Preaching is theology coming through a man who is on fire." Do you burn within? Does the

Word of God burn within you when you study it, or do you just find yourself "doing sermons?" There is an anointing that comes in the very moment of preaching Christ. It is an anointing that the apostles speak of repeatedly. In the book of Acts you find repeated references to the fullness of the Spirit, and to boldness. That word group that is used consistently for "boldness" is the word that most describes what happens when the power of the Spirit came upon these these preachers. What is it that He gave them? He gave them an elocution that burned within them with such effect upon the hearers that they heard, as the Thessalonian epistle says, not the word of man but the very Word of God.

I am no friend of what is popularly called "neo-orthodoxy," but I have heard more from some early neo-orthodox writers about the preaching that illumines Christ than I have from 20th-century arid, intellectually orthodox, evangelicals. This was the same tradition that was there in the Reformers; it was there in the Puritans, but it has been lost in our day, especially in terms of how we connect reason and logic with fire in the Spirit and the ministry of the Word. No wonder people run from place to place looking for an "experience," when the kind of preaching that we often give them, we say to our shame, is only intellectual, systematic theologizing.

We need the Spirit of God more than we know if we are to speak to the minds of our hearers. Think of the opposition. Think of what you are up against week by week. Our people are bombarded with the amusement culture. They are bombarded with things that entertain them and put them in a state of non-thinking. And then after 163 hours of this kind of culture and life they are supposed to make a quick transition to being thinking Christians? Think of the challenge you've got! Who is sufficient, in the light of all of this? Who is able? The man of God who is set on fire with the truth of God, who believes that he is called by God and equipped by the Spirit of God to speak to the minds of his hearers in such a compelling way that he must have an audience. He must be heard because his theme is so great and his message is true. May God equip holy ministers to preach the truth to the minds of their hearers so that they hear Christ, and Him as crucified.

Preaching to the Heart

Sinclair B. Ferguson

No more poignant or instructive description of the work of the minister of the gospel exists than Paul's "defensive excursus"[1] in 2 Corinthians 2:14–7:4. Every Christian preacher should aim to possess a good working knowledge of this seminal part of the New Testament. For Paul simultaneously describes and defends his service as an apostle of Jesus Christ and a minister of the New Covenant. He uses this language explicitly when he affirms: "God has made us competent as ministers of a new covenant" (2 Corinthians 3:6). In what follows he takes us from the outside of his ministry to its deep internal roots (2 Corinthians 4:1–18)

> Therefore, since through God's mercy we have this ministry, we do not lose heart. Rather, we have renounced secret and shameful ways; we do not use deception, nor do we distort the word of God. On the contrary, by setting forth the truth plainly we commend ourselves to every man's conscience in the sight of God. And even if our gospel is veiled, it is

---

[1] The expression is that of Paul Barnett, *The Second Epistle to the Corinthians* (Grand Rapids, Mich.: Eerdmans, 1997), 210.

veiled to those who are perishing. The god of this age has blinded the minds of unbelievers, so that they cannot see the light of the gospel of the glory of Christ, who is the image of God. For we do not preach ourselves, but Jesus Christ as Lord, and ourselves as your servants for Jesus' sake. For God, who said, "Let light shine out of darkness," made his light shine in our hearts to give us the light of the knowledge of the glory of God in the face of Christ.

But we have this treasure in jars of clay to show that this all-surpassing power is from God and not from us. We are hard pressed on every side, but not crushed; perplexed, but not in despair; persecuted, but not abandoned; struck down, but not destroyed. We always carry around in our body the death of Jesus, so that the life of Jesus may also be revealed in our body. For we who are alive are always being given over to death for Jesus' sake, so that His life may be revealed in our mortal body. So then, death is at work in us, but life is at work in you.

It is written, "I believed, therefore I have spoken." With that same spirit of faith we also believe and therefore speak, because we know that the one who raised the Lord Jesus from the dead will also raise us with Jesus and present us with you in his presence. All this is for your benefit, so that the grace that is reaching more and more people may cause thanksgiving to overflow to the glory of God.

Therefore we do not lose heart. Though outwardly we are wasting away, yet inwardly we are being renewed day by day. For our light and momentary troubles are achieving for us an eternal glory that far outweighs them all. So we fix our eyes not on what is

seen, but what is unseen. For what is seen is temporary, but what is unseen is eternal.

The title of this chapter is "Preaching to the
Heart." All truly biblical preaching is preaching to
the heart; but what do we mean when speak of
preaching to the heart?

The Heart

In Scripture "the heart" only rarely denotes the
physical organ. Characteristically it refers to the
central core of the individual's being and personality: the deep-seated element of a person that provides both the energy and the drive for all of the
faculties (e.g., Deuteronomy 4:9; Matthew 12:34). It
denotes the governing center of life.

Interestingly, of the 858 occurrences of the
Hebrew terms for heart, *leb* and *lebab*, almost all
have reference to human beings (in distinction
from either God or other creatures). Indeed "heart"
is the Old Testament's major anthropological
term.[2]

Modern Westerners tend to think of the heart as
the center of a person's emotional life (hence its
use as the symbol of romantic rather than volitional love). But the Hebrew conceptualization

---

2 H. W. Wolff, *Anthropology of the Old Testament*, trans. M.
Kohl (London: SCM Press, 1974), 40–55.

placed the emotion-center lower in the anatomy, and located the intellectual energy center of the human person in the heart. Hence "heart" is frequently used as a synonym for the mind, the will, and the conscience, as well as (on occasion) for the affections. It refers to the fundamental bent or characteristic of an individual's life.

In this sense, when we think about speaking or preaching to the heart, we do not have in view directly addressing the emotions as such. In any event, as Jonathan Edwards argued with such force, the mind cannot be so easily bypassed. Rather we are thinking of preaching that influences the very core and center of an individual's being and makes an impact on the whole person, including the emotions—but does so primarily by instructing and appealing to the mind. Such a focus is of paramount importance for preachers because the transformation and the renewal of the heart is what is chiefly in view in their proclamation of the gospel (cf. Romans 12:1-2).

This is, in fact, already implied in Paul's description of himself and his companions as "competent ministers of a new covenant" (2 Corinthians 3:6). Built into the foundation of the New Covenant is the promise of a transformed heart:

> I will sprinkle clean water on you, and you will be clean. I will cleanse you from all your impurities and

from all your idols. I will give you a new heart I
will remove from you your heart of stone and give
you a heart of flesh (Ezekiel 36:25–26).

No matter under what circumstances we preach
the Word of God, no matter to whom we are speaking, insofar as we too are called to be "competent
ministers of the new covenant," our preaching must
always have the heart in view.

Threefold Openness

Paul speaks more fully here about his own
preaching ministry than anywhere else in the New
Testament. One of the keynotes he strikes is that
preaching to the heart is marked by an openness of
a threefold character.

1. It involves an openness of Paul's being, a
transparency before God. "What we are," he says,
"is plain to God" (2 Corinthians 5:11).

2. It also implies an opening out of the love that
fills his heart toward the people to whom he is
ministering. "We ourselves have opened our hearts
wide to you Corinthians" (2 Corinthians 6:11).

3. Within that twofold context—his own heart
opened vertically toward God and horizontally
toward those to whom he is seeking to minister—
Paul's preaching to the heart is also characterized
by an opening up of the truth. He expresses this in
an illuminating way when he describes it as "set-

ting forth the truth plainly" (2 Corinthians 4:2),
what the King James Version describes more
graphically as "the open manifestation of the
truth."

Thus, just as he is an open book in the sight of
God, similarly the preacher lays open the integrity
of his life to the consciences and hearts of his hearers as though he were a letter to be read by them
(cf. 2 Corinthians 3:2).

But these characteristics are never isolated from
the way in which we handle the Scriptures, opening up and laying bare their message in both exposition and application. The Corinthians had already seen these hallmarks in Paul's ministry. They
were a large part of the explanation for its power
and fruit. They are no less essential to the minister
of the gospel today if he is to preach with similar
effect on the hearts of his hearers.

Preaching to the heart, then, is not merely a matter of technique or homiletic method or style. These
things have their proper place and relevance. But
the more fundamental, indeed, essential thing for
the preacher is surely the fact that something has
happened to his own heart; it has been laid bare
before God by His Word. He, in turn, lays it bare in
his ministry before those to whom he ministers.
And within that two-fold personal context, the goal
he has in view is so to lay bare the truth of the

Word of God that the hearts of those who hear are opened vertically to God and horizontally to one another.

Paul had already reflected on this impact of God's Word in 1 Corinthians 14, in the context of his discussion of tongues and prophecy in the Corinthian church.

Prophetic utterance always possesses an element of speaking "to the heart" (Isaiah 40:2).[3] Through such preaching even someone who comes in from the outside finds that "the secrets of his heart will be laid bare. So he will fall down and worship God, exclaiming 'God is really among you' " (1 Corinthians 14:24–25).

In the last analysis, this is what preaching to the heart is intended to produce: inner prostration of the hearts of our listeners through a consciousness of the presence and the glory of God. This distinguishes authentic biblical, expository preaching from any cheap substitute for it; it marks the difference between preaching about the Word of God and preaching the Word of God.

The presence of this threefold cord, then, is a great desideratum in expository preaching. When there is the exposition of the Scriptures, an enlarging and opening of the preacher's heart, and the

---

[3] "Speak tenderly" (Isaiah 40:2, NIV; ESV) is, literally, "speak to (or, upon) the heart" (cf. Genesis 34:3; Hosea 2:14).

exposing of the hearts of the hearers, then the majesty of the Word of God written will be self-evident and the presence of the Word of God Incarnate will stand forth in all His glory.

Man Small, God Great

There is a widespread need for this kind of preaching. We have an equal need as preachers to catch the vision for it in an overly pragmatic and programmatic society that believes it is possible to live the Christian life without either the exposing of our own hearts or the accompanying prostration of ourselves before the majesty of God on high.

It is just here that one notices a striking contrast between the biblical exposition one finds in the steady preaching of John Calvin in the 16th century and preaching in our own day. It is clearly signaled by the words with which he ended virtually every one of his thousands of sermons: "And now let us bow down before the majesty of our gracious God. . . ." Reformation biblical exposition made God great and man bow down. By contrast, much modern preaching seems to have as its goal making man feel great, even if God Himself has to bow down.

So a leading characteristic of preaching to the heart will be the humbling, indeed, the prostration of hearts before the majesty of God on high. This is simultaneously the true ecstasy of the Christian, and therein lies the paradox of grace: the way down is always the way up.

Such exposition of the Scriptures, of oneself, of our hearers' hearts is a far more demanding task in the gospel ministry than providing psychological wisdom which people can then fit into their already well-supported lives.

But if, through the preaching of the gospel, we want to see people prostrated with mingled awe and joy before God, the essential prerequisite is that we ourselves have first of all been prostrated before him. John Owen's words still ring true even after three and a half centuries: "a man preacheth that sermon only well unto others which preacheth itself in his own soul . . . . If the word do not dwell with power *in* us, it will not pass with power *from* us."[4]

Preaching to the heart—through whatever personality, in whatever style—will always exhibit the following five characteristics:

1. A Right Use of the Bible

Preaching to the heart is undergirded by our familiarity with the use of sacred Scripture.

---

[4] John Owen, *The True Nature of a Gospel Church,* in *The Works of John Owen,* ed. W. H. Goold (Edinburgh, 1853), 16:76. This has been reprinted by the Banner of Truth Trust.

According to 2 Timothy 3:16, all Scripture is useful (*ophelimōs*) for certain practical functions: for teaching; for rebuking; for correcting; for training in righteousness, so that the man of God may be thoroughly equipped for every good work.

If it were not for the fact that a chapter division appears in our Bibles at this point (giving the impression that Paul is now changing gears in his charge to Timothy), we would not so easily have missed the point implicit in what he goes on to say: "Timothy, if that's what the Bible is for, use it that way!" For in 2 Timothy 4:1–2 he takes up these same uses of Scripture (teaching, rebuking, correcting, encouraging in godly living) and applies them. In effect, he says to Timothy, "Use the God-breathed Scriptures this way in your ministry!"

Those who love the richer, older theology of the Reformation and Puritan eras, and of Jonathan Edwards and Thomas Boston, may be tempted to look askance at the modern Professor of Preaching as he hands out copies of his "preaching grid" to the incoming class of freshmen taking Homiletics 101. But the fact is that here we find Paul handing out the last copy of his own "preaching grid" to Timothy! This is by no means the only preaching grid to be found, either in Scripture or in the Reformed tradition.[5] But it certainly is a grid that

---

[5] I am thinking here of our Lord's "grid" in the parable of the

ought to be built into our basic approach to preaching.

Thus informed, we come to see that preaching
to the heart will give expression to four things: instruction in the truth, conviction of the conscience,
restoration and transformation of life,[6] and equipping for service.[7] Let us not think that we have
gained so much maturity in Christian living and
service that we can bypass the fundamental structures that the apostles give us to help us practically
in these areas.

Preaching, therefore, involves teaching—imparting doctrine in order to renew and transform the
mind. It implies the inevitable rebuke of our sin,
and brings with it the healing of divine correction.

The language of "correction" (*epanorthōsis*) is
used in the Septuagint for the rebuilding of a city
or the repair of a sanctuary.[8] Outside of biblical

---

sower and the soils (Mark 4:1–20), and of the seminal work of
the early English Puritan William Perkins, *The Arte of
Prophecying* (Latin 1592, English 1606).

[6] *Epanorthōsis:* correction here carries the positive connota-
tion of "restoration."

[7] *Exertismenōs:* the same root (*artizō*) is used of the goal of the
ministry of the Word in Ephesians 4:12 and of the disciples
washing, mending, and preparing their nets in Mark 1:19.

[8] See Çeslas Spicq, *Theological Lexicon of the New Testament,*
trans. and ed. James D. Ernest (Peabody, Mass.:
Hendrickson, 1994), 2:30–31.

Greek, it is used in the medical textbooks of the ancient world for setting broken limbs. It is a word that belongs to the world of reconstruction, remedy, healing, and restoration. So we find here too another characteristic of the Apostle Paul: a masterful balance between the negation of sin and the up-building of the Christian believer, "in order that the man of God may be thoroughly equipped for every good work." If we are going to preach to the heart, then our preaching will always (admittedly in different kinds of balance) be characterized by these four marks of authenticity.

But such preaching must first be directed to the mind. When we preach to the heart we are not engaged in rebuking the conscience or cleansing the emotions directly. Rather preaching to the heart addresses the understanding first, in order to instruct it; but in doing so it also reaches through the mind to inform, rebuke, and cleanse the conscience. It then touches the will in order to reform and transform life and equip the saints for the work of ministry (Ephesians 4:12).

When we preach to the heart, the mind is not so much the terminus of our preaching, but the channel through which we appeal to the whole person, and the fulcrum that, once renewed, leads to the transformation of the whole life.

2. Nourishment of the Whole Person

There is an important balance to be pursued here of ministering to the understanding, affections, and will. It is very easy to lose sight of this. Its significance may perhaps best be underlined by means of a personal illustration.

Many years ago, I had the privilege of preaching on a few occasions in a particular congregation. During this period (and with no connection between these facts!) the pastor of the church received and accepted a call to serve elsewhere. Friends whom I made during these occasional visits confided in me some time after the departure of their pastor (to whom they were extremely loyal): "As we have sought to assess the impact of these last years of ministry on our lives, we have come to this conclusion: while we were thoroughly well-instructed, we were poorly nourished."

There is a difference between these two things: a well-instructed congregation and a well-nourished one (just as there often is a difference between a well-instructed congregation and a well-educated one). It is possible to instruct, yet fail to nourish those to whom we preach. It is possible to address the mind, but to do so with little concern to see the conscience, the heart, and the affections reached and cleansed, the will redirected and the whole person transformed through a renewed mind. By contrast, in this picture of preaching first painted for Timothy, Paul is teaching us how to preach to the heart in a way that will nourish the whole person.

Pathos

One of the characteristics of such preaching is pathos, the stimulation in us of a sense of sadness, even broken-heartedness.

Pathos is not mere emotion for its own sake, certainly not the kind of emotionalism that tends to descend into bathos. In preaching it is, rather, the communication and evoking through our words of the responsive "mood" appropriate to sinners listening to the gospel we are preaching. In this way our listeners become aware of the power of the truths we are preaching about human sin and divine grace and glory.

The great Welsh preacher Dr. D. Martyn Lloyd-Jones on one occasion made a fascinating and illuminating (to me, at least) self-critical comment on what he felt had been a weaknesses of his own preaching ministry. He thought that it had lacked in at least one particular aspect—pathos.

Christians of an earlier time sometimes spoke of sermons as "pathetic." We, of course, would not cross the road to hear preaching if it was "pathetic" in the modern sense of the word! But our forefa-

thers meant something quite different by this expression, namely, preaching which leaves its hearers with melted hearts. Why? Because the preaching has come from a similarly broken and melted
heart that has already placed itself under this four-
fold applicatory grid of Scripture: the preaching
heart has been instructed by the truth of Scripture;
the conscience rebuked by the holiness of Scripture;
the spirit nourished by the correction, healing, and
restorative power of the truth of Scripture. Thus the
man of God, the preacher, is equipped to speak
God's Word from his own heart to our hearts.

3. Understanding the Condition of the Hearers

Preaching to the heart always reflects an awareness of the actual condition of our hearers. In one
form or another most preaching manuals under-
score this point. The preacher emerges from the
world of the biblical text to speak in the name of
Christ to the world of his hearers.

One of the hidden snares in systematic biblical
preaching is that we may become so taken up with
the task of studying and explaining the text that
we forget the actual poverty and falsehood it addresses. One—distinctively Reformed—manifestation of this is for a love for the works of the past
(coupled with their ready availability today!), our
discovery (for example) of the depth of Puritan
preaching by comparison with contemporary

preaching, to suck us in to the very language and speech patterns of a past era, thus making us sound inauthentic to our own generation.

By contrast, preaching to the heart will not be encrusted with layers of ill-digested materials from the past, however relevant these were to their own day. Those preaching helps must rather be thoroughly digested by us, made our own, and applied to people today in today's language. That is what it means to bring the truth to bear upon men and women, and boys and girls, in such a way that it opens up and penetrates into their hearts.

In this sense, biblical exposition must speak to the people sitting today in the pews, not to those who sat in them hundred of years ago!

This in fact is one of the cardinal principles expounded by William Perkins in his great work, *The Arte of Prophecying* (sic), the original Puritan manual on preaching.

Perkins argues that we have to understand the soul-condition of those to whom we preach, and address them in an appropriate and relevant way.

Whenever we preach, we have people in a whole series of different spiritual conditions listening to us. Perkins realized that if he was going to touch them with the truth of the gospel, then he must—always in a way that is consistent with that gospel—shape appropriately the presentation and

application of the truth. Only thus will it serve as a
sharp instrument to hand to the Holy Spirit, the
Divine Surgeon, in order that He may cut open the
hearts of the people and bring healing to their dis-
eased spirits. In that sense, the shape of our exposition of Scripture can never be abstracted from the
characteristics and shape of those to whom we
preach it.

Perkins' own grid is inherently interesting—and
valuable, if one employs it in a way that makes it
genuinely one's own. He suggests that preaching
should be shaped to seven categories of hearers:

Non-Christians who know nothing about the
gospel and have unteachable spirits.

Non-Christians who know nothing about the
gospel but who are teachable.

Those who know what the gospel is but who
have never been humbled to see their need of a
Savior.

Those who have been humbled, some in the
early stages of seeing their need, others who see
that they need salvation, not merely improvement,
and are now convinced that only Christ can save
them.

Genuine believers who need to be taught.

Backsliders, either because of (a) a failure to
understand the gospel clearly, or (b) a failure to
live consistently with it.

A mixed congregation of believers and unbelievers—which Perkins regards as the norm most preachers encounter.[9]

But we do not need to appeal to the Puritans for the authority to operate with such a grid providing us with a general categorization of hearers; our Lord Jesus did so Himself. On at least one occasion He divided His hearers into four different categories and likened them to the receptivity or otherwise of different kinds of soil to seed sown in it: the pathway, the rocky soil, the weed-infested soil, and the good soil (Mark 4:1–20).

It would make for a fascinating academic study of the ministry of Jesus to take this parable of the sower, the seed, and the soils as a lens through which to examine, categorize, and analyze His preaching. For preachers, too, it is a fruitful exercise to consider the ways in which He applied His message to the four different spiritual conditions to which He saw Himself speaking.

Is it because expository preaching is such a demanding activity, and we are so consumed by its demands, that some of us pay so little attention (or

---

[9] William Perkins, *The Arte of Prophecying* (Latin 1592, English 1606) in *The Works of William Perkins,* vol. 2 (London, 1617), 665–668. For an edited and modernized version, see *The Art of Prophesying,* ed. S. B. Ferguson (Edinburgh: Banner of Truth Trust, 1996), 56–63.

at least too little attention) to the spiritual condition of those to whom we are preaching? If so, we need to reconsider our approach.

If it is important that we learn to know the condition of the hearts of our hearers, the best place to begin is, of course, with our own hearts. Apply the Word there, and we will soon learn to be like surgical attendants: our exposition of the text will become like sterilized knives, perfectly tooled, which we hand to the Spirit for the precise spiritual surgery that our people actually need.

A further feature that characterized our Lord Jesus' preaching was that the common people heard Him gladly (Mark 12:37). We ought not to dismiss this with the cheap comment that they soon changed their tune. For they immediately and instinctively recognized the difference between the book learning and authority-citing style of the scribes and the applied biblical wisdom and heart-knowledge displayed in Jesus' preaching. The scribes and teachers of the law spoke about the Bible in a manner removed from daily experience. Jesus, in stark contrast, seemed to speak from inside the Bible in a way that addressed their hearts.

Sadly, some of our preaching carries with it the atmosphere of being "about the Bible" rather than conveying a sense that here the Bible is speaking, and indeed God Himself is speaking. This will be changed only when we come to Scripture in the spirit of the Servant of the Lord:

"The Sovereign Lord has given me an instructed tongue, to know the word that sustains the weary. He wakens me morning by morning, wakens my ear to listen like one being taught. The Sovereign Lord has opened my ears, and I have not been rebellious; I have not drawn back" (Isaiah 50:4–5).

4. *The Use of the Imagination*

Preaching to the heart is aided by our recognition of what our task really is. The great question is: How, through the work of the Spirit, am I best to get the Word of God into the hearts of the people?

Those who have done, or today do this with greatest fruitfulness and success are marked by many gifts and characteristics, often very diverse. But one thing all of them seem to have in common is imagination—an imaginative creativity that bridges the distance between the truth of the Word of God and the lives of those to whom they speak.

In some preachers this is most evident in the imaginative power of their illustrations. In the case of George Whitefield, his use of illustrations was sometimes so vivid and real that people thought they were actually so caught up in the events he was describing as to confuse what they were hearing with reality.

By contrast, the congregation of St. Peter's Church in Geneva listened to John Calvin, week in and week out (and sometimes virtually daily), preaching an average of five 40 minute sermons a week during the course of his lengthy ministry, but with virtually no stories or illustrations of that kind.

Like most of us, Calvin did not possess Whitfield's imaginative power (nor his magical voice!). Nevertheless his sermons *lived* and had the power to stir young men to be willing to suffer martyrdom for Christ. For Calvin had an ability to use language with such imaginative power that his preaching bridged the gap between life in ancient Judah and Israel and life in 16th-century Geneva, Switzerland. He expressed and applied the truth in a way that was saturated in the language of the daily life of his hearers, bringing the Word of God right into the nitty-gritty practicalities of their experience.

Similarly, Richard Baxter preached in such a way that his sermons so connected with life in 17th- century Kidderminster, England, that the truth he spoke exploded during the week like time bombs planted in his congregation's memories.

The Spirit is well able to use different sets of imaginative skills, employed in different contexts, producing similar effects. But clearly the ability to imagine the Word being taken from the Scriptures and screwed into the minds of the hearers is common to all lively exposition.

Scripture itself employs different metaphors to help us grasp how important it is thus to "see ourselves into" the hearts and situations of those to whom we preach. Here are some drawn simply at random. The preacher is a sower of seed; a teacher of students; a father of children; a mother giving birth; a nurse feeding infants; a shepherd, rescuing and caring for the sheep of the flock; a soldier engaged in warfare; and a builder constructing the temple of God.

We need only to think of ourselves in terms of these metaphors to see what is involved in bringing the Word of God to bear upon the hearts and consciences of those to whom we are preaching. What does a farmer do? He sows the seed and plows the ground. He prayerfully waits for its fruition. What does a builder do? He clears a building site and erects the building. What does a shepherd do? He feeds and protects his flock. How, then, can I get the seed into this soil? How can I clear the site and chisel this stone into shape? How can I prepare this meal for these people?

In these different ways we come to recognize what it means to be a preacher. Our own imagination is fired and we begin to learn how to preach to the heart.

5. *Grace in Christ*

The fifth key to fruitful preaching to the heart is the preacher's own grasp of the principle and the reality of grace. This needs to be set within the multi-faceted context of a growing familiarity with the uses of sacred Scripture, of an awareness of the actual condition of our hearers, and a conscious recognition of what the task of the preacher is. But always the melody line of preaching to the heart lies in our own grasp of the principle of grace. That is what makes preaching "sing," and it applies to both the content and the manner of our preaching.

It applies to the *content* of our preaching. Only the preaching of grace can open the sinful heart. Unaided law, imperatives without indicatives, cannot pry open locked hearts. It is grace, and—yes—the preaching of the law in the context of grace, expounding the grace of law, that opens the heart. This is the very point John Newton so famously made in the best-known of his Olney Hymns, "Amazing Grace":

'Twas grace that taught my heart to fear,
And grace my fears relieved.

Paul stressed this to the Corinthians. The heart and soul of his ministry was: "I resolved to know nothing while I was with you except Jesus Christ and Him crucified" (1 Corinthians 2:2). Through such preaching there was a *phanerosis,* a manifestation ("setting forth," 2 Corinthians 4:2, NIV) of the truth, a making known of what he calls "the light of the gospel of the glory of Christ who is the image of God" (4:4). For when "Jesus Christ as Lord" is thus manifested in preaching, God again makes "his light shine in our hearts to give us the light of the knowledge of the glory of God in the face of Christ" (4:6).

A caveat is in order here, which is particularly relevant to a time like our own when the ancient patristic and reformation style of consecutive exposition (the *lectio continua* method) has undergone something of a revival. We must never make the mistake of thinking that any system of consecutive exposition of Scripture absolutely guarantees the preaching of Christ.

It is possible naively to assume, because we are preaching in a systematic way through books of the Bible, that we are therefore inevitably preaching Christ and Him crucified. That ought to be the case, but is not necessarily so. Sadly, one may preach in a consecutive way through the Bible without preaching in a truly Christocentric way. Indeed, paradoxically, one may have a passion for preaching the Bible without having a passion for preaching Christ and Him crucified.

Hints of this can be seen in the fact that evangelical Christians (who write the bulk of Christian books, preach more sermons, sponsor more conferences and seminars, broadcast more TV and radio programs) actually write few books, sponsor few seminars and seldom arrange conferences or devote airtime to the theme of Jesus Christ and Him crucified.

In addition to this, we may even major on the theme of grace in a way that is disconnected from Christ Himself, treating it as a commodity and losing sight of the fact that it can be found only through a Person.

There is a center to the Bible and its message of grace. It is found in Jesus Christ crucified and resurrected. Grace must therefore be preached in a way that is centered and focused on Jesus Christ Himself, never offering the benefits of the gospel without the Benefactor Himself.

For many preachers, however, it is much easier to deal with the pragmatic things; even to expose and denounce sin, to answer the "how to" questions, than it is to give an adequate explanation of the source of the forgiveness, acceptance, and power we need in order "how to."

We see this lack in the teaching, preaching, and the literature of our day. We give our best and most creative energies to teaching God's people almost everything except the person and work of our Lord and Savior. If this is true, it should cause us considerable alarm. For there is reason to fear that our failure here has reached epidemic proportions.

We need to return to a true preaching to the heart, rooted in the principle of grace and focused on the person of the Lord Jesus Christ. Then people will not say about our ministry merely, "he is an expository preacher"; or "that was practical," nor even "he cuts open our consciences"; but instead, "he preached Christ to me, and his preaching was directed to my conscience. It was evident that he gave the best of his intellectual skills and the warmth of his compassion and emotion to thinking about, living for, and proclaiming his beloved Savior, Jesus Christ." This is what will reach the heart! And when you have experienced such preaching, or seen its fruit, you know what true preaching is. And you know that its fruit lasts for all eternity.

But this principle of grace in Christ applies also to the *manner* of our preaching.

Even today, 160 years after his early death, when we read the memoirs or the sermons of someone like Robert Murray M'Cheyne, we can still feel the power that must have gripped people as his preaching reached into their hearts.

On the morning of M'Cheyne's death a letter of gratitude for what turned out to be the last sermon he ever preached reached him. It was left unopened on his desk, and he never read the words of a grateful listener who commented, "It was not so much what you said as the manner in which you said it."

This is a major key to reaching the heart in preaching. For while preaching involves bringing the world of the Bible to bear upon the world of our contemporaries, it also involves bringing the message-in-words of the Scriptures through the message-in-manner of the preacher.

There needs to be a marriage between the message and the manner. Therein lies the heart of the mystery of preaching. As our hearts are opened wide to the grace of God in the gospel, and simultaneously opened wide to our hearers, the power of the gospel is set on display (see 2 Corinthians 6:11).

Paul expresses this memorably in 2 Corinthians 4:5: "We do not preach ourselves, but Jesus Christ as Lord." But there is a corollary to this: "We ourselves are your bondslaves for Jesus' sake."

The evidence that I preach Jesus Christ as Lord is found not so much in my declarations as it is in the manifestation of that Lordship in my life and preaching—when I, who am His bondslave, am willing to be and actually become in my preaching, the bondslave of others for Jesus' sake.

In the last analysis, preaching to the heart is preaching Christ in a way that reminds people of Christ, but also manifests Christ to them, and draws them to Him. If, among other things, preaching is (as Phillips Brooks's famous description claims) "the bringing of truth through personality,"[10] then the personalities of the preachers of the cross must be marked by the cross. So we are called to be cruciformed (shaped by the cross), Christophers (bearing the Christ of the cross), and Christplacarders (setting Christ and Him crucified on display, cf. Galatians 3:1) in our preaching as we "try to persuade men" (2 Corinthians 5:11).

Perhaps such preaching of Christ is less common than we assume. If so, it is because we do not know Him nearly well enough.   Let us, then, resolve that, above all other ambitions, we will know Him, the power of His resurrection, and the fellowship of His sufferings (Philippians 3:10). Let us also be determined to know nothing but Jesus Christ and Him crucified (1 Corinthians 2:2), so that, as we preach to the heart, God Himself will speak to His people heart to heart.

---

[10] Phillips Brooks, *Lectures on Preaching* (London, n.d., first published in London in 1877), 5.

Preaching with Authority

Don Kistler

"The result was that when Jesus had finished these words, the multitudes were amazed at His teaching; for He was teaching them as one having authority, and not as their scribes."   Matthew 7:28–29

Jesus must have been an amazing preacher, because the Scripture tells us that when He preached people were amazed, which would make Him an amazing preacher. But what was the source of their amazement? He taught as one who had authority, *not* like the scribes and Pharisees.

It is to be feared that we have far too many scribes and Pharisees in pulpits today. They do not preach with authority and the people are not amazed—amused, perhaps, but not amazed. Nowadays preachers make suggestions; they do not preach with authority. We hear things like, "I think that what God is suggesting here is this. . . ." But God doesn't make suggestions. He gives commands. He did not give us the Ten Suggestions. One comedian has said that in his church they have 6 commandments and 4 "do-the-best-you-can's." That may be funny, but it is not biblical.

Jesus preached with authority. Why? Because He had authority! And the preachers of old preached with authority. They preached, "Thus saith the Lord." We have lost that today, I'm afraid. Our preaching reflects it and the lives of our people reflect it as well. They live as if the pastor had no authority, as if the elders had no authority, and, even more appalling, as if the Word of God itself had no authority. We have returned to the place of the church in the Old Testament where "every man did what was right in his own eyes." It is true today; every man thinks what is right in his own mind, regardless of what Scripture or sound exegesis may say otherwise.

Paul was a firm believer in the authority of the pulpit. When he wrote to Titus, in 2:15, he wrote, "These things speak and exhort and reprove with all authority. Let no one disregard you." And the things that Titus was to speak with authority are things most preachers wouldn't dream of addressing: women subjecting themselves to their husbands; women staying at home with their children—but Titus was to preach those things with authority! Titus was not to suggest, cajole, entice, or stroke his people. He was to convince the people of the truth of what he was saying. All these are in the command mode. He was to, as Richard Baxter said, "Screw the truth into men's minds." The word for authority here is "command." Preach in the command mode, Titus. That's what Paul is saying.

It is nearly the same as what he wrote to Timothy in 2 Timothy 4:1–2: "I solemnly charge you in the presence of God and of Christ Jesus, who is to judge the living and the dead, and by His appearing and His kingdom, preach the Word; be ready in season and out of season." How was Timothy to preach? "Reprove, rebuke, exhort, with great patience and instruction." The word for instruction is *didache.* Teach them patiently, but teach them. Teach them something!

In Jeremiah 3:15, God defined a preacher's call: "I will give them pastors after My own heart." What a calling! What is it to be a pastor after God's own heart? What would grant a man such a designation? A great bedside manner? Excellent people skills? Visitation in triple digits? No, it is none of those things. "I will give them pastors after My own heart, who shall feed them with knowledge and understanding." That's what makes a man a pastor after God's own heart. He feeds God's people with knowledge and understanding. Doctrine and application. What to do and how to do it! Knowledge and practice!

Was that not the call Christ gave to Peter? "If you love Me," what? "Feed My sheep!" There was an article some years ago in the now-defunct *National and International Religion Report* about the moving of the Spirit of God among the Navajo Indians in our country. One of their spokesmen said that if someone tried to preach for 20 minutes, he would be thrown out. "They don't come to leave empty," he said.

I have a dear friend who often supplies the pulpit in a local black church in Pittsburgh. His first time there was an eye-opener for him. He was introduced to speak after an hour and 40 minutes. He asked his host how long he had to preach. The response was, "Till you're done, brother; we didn't come here to leave!" How would you like to have that group to work with!

At this point, here come the objections; but Paul has already anticipated them. 2 Timothy 4:3–4: "For the time will come when they will not endure sound doctrine; but, wanting to have their ears tickled, they will accumulate for themselves teachers in accordance with their own desires; and will turn away their ears from the truth, and will turn aside to myths."

A pastor might say, "That's the problem. My people won't take that from me. There would be a mutiny if I preached like that!"

But what does Paul say? "But you, be sober in all things, endure hardship, do the work of an evangelist, fulfill your ministry." Do you see what he is saying? Your calling hasn't changed because the group dynamics of your congregation has changed! You don't change just because they don't like it! You are preaching to please the Lord, not your people! Your calling is from Him; it is His approval that matters. It is He who will declare (or will not declare) "Well done, thou good and faithful servant."

We can preach with authority because Christ has given us that authority. Did He not say, "All authority has been given to Me in heaven and earth. Go therefore and make disciples of all nations . . . teaching them to observe all that I have commanded you." It wasn't "teaching them to observe all that I have *suggested* to you," but "all that I have *commanded* you"!

Romans 10 gives us a picture of Paul's pastoral heart. He states that his heart's desire for the people is their salvation. Any pastor who feels differently is not a faithful minister of Jesus Christ. I remember when the presbytery committee on evangelism came to the church I was pastoring and asked what we were doing evangelistically. My response was that we were trying to get some of our members saved! I wasn't kidding; my heart's desire for my congregation was that they get saved.

Then Paul begins to reveal the process by which God ordinarily is pleased to save souls. In verse 13

he declares that whoever shall call upon the name
of the Lord shall be saved. But the question is then
asked, "How then shall they call upon Him in
whom they have not believed?" Then, as we come to
the next verse, the translators must have felt that
since there was a preposition before "Him" in verse
13 that there must be a need for one in verse 14—
"of whom"—but there is none in the original. "How
shall they believe in Him *whom* they have not
heard. And how shall they hear without a
preacher? And how shall they preach unless they
are sent?"

There are some very pertinent questions here.
"How shall they believe in Him whom they have
not heard? And how shall they hear without a
preacher?" The question is not asked how they
shall hear *about* Him, but how shall they hear Him
without a preacher! Do you get what Paul is saying
here? When the faithful minister is properly exegeting the Word of God, it is God Himself who is
speaking to His people! Failure to hear the faithful
minister is a failure to hear God Himself!

Isn't that exactly what Jesus told His disciples?
"If they won't listen to you, they won't listen to Me!"
That is why we are not to let anyone disregard us,
because that would mean that we are letting them
disregard Christ! "How shall they hear Christ without a preacher?" That is the question! A faithful

minister is the mouthpiece of God!

Preachers are one of the love gifts of the ascended Christ to His body, the church. Never let anyone denigrate the sacred calling a pastor has to stand in his pulpit and faithfully exegete the inspired Word of God to the people of God, thereby making himself the mouthpiece of God!

Pastors must deliver God's Word to His people in such a manner that the majesty and authority of it is preserved. Have you ever noticed that whenever in Scripture the Bible is read, all the people were standing out of reverence? What do we do today? We sit! Why is that? Why do we not stand as well out of reverence for God's Word?

And why do preachers often act as if what they are saying is simply their opinion? Preachers are not there to give their opinions, they are supposed to be giving the people the very mind of God! Failure to do so was a mark of the false prophets in Jeremiah's day. "The prophets prophesy on their own authority; and My people love it so." The people love it when no one is in charge. They love it when the pastor is on the same level as they are. They love it when they share; they don't love it when pastors preach.

Any other time of of a man's life, he is on the same level as his people are; but when he mounts the pulpit, he becomes something else entirely.

A preacher is just a sinner saved by grace. But, like everything else, when God sets a common thing apart for a sacred use, it is for that time no longer a common thing. Grape juice is just grape juice until it is consecrated in Lord's Supper, and then it is something else again!

When Jesus preached, He didn't wait for someone to validate His message or authority. He said His "verily, verily" at the beginning of the message, not at the end. What he said wasn't open for debate. Too often preachers give their people the impression that all they need to do is think about what has been said. How many times have you heard: "Well, pastor, you've given me a lot to think about." Fine, think about it and then do it. God never gave us His Word to think about, God gave us His Word to obey! Or some think they are just to talk about the sermon. Thomas Watson says in a sermon entitled "Knowing and Doing," in the collection of sermons called *A Plea for the Godly,* that if God had meant His Word to be talked about, He'd have given it to parrots!

Preachers must preach for conviction and change. No one ought ever to leave a sermon without having a very real sense that there is something in their lives they need to do something about. They may say, "I'm not going to do that!" But they ought never to leave a sermon saying, "I don't

know what I'm supposed to do with that information." Shame on ministers if they do!

Remember, however, that any authority ministers have is a granted or delegated authority.
Christ's authority is inherent; the Author has the
authority. Ministers have no inherent authority; it is
all derived. So, in that sense, a minister cannot imitate His authority, but he can imitate His zeal, His
boldness. That is what Paul asked the people to
pray for regarding him in Ephesians, that he would
proclaim with boldness the mystery of the gospel.

Thomas Taylor said, "A flattering ministry is an
enemy to this authority; for when a minister must
sing placebos and sweet songs, it is impossible for
him not to betray the truth. To withstand this authority, or to weaken it, is a fearful sin, whether in
high or low men; and the Lord will not allow His
messengers feet to be cut off." Now if that is a sin
in the people, how much more a sin do you think
it is for the messenger himself to do it?!

Preach the Word! Don't preach the latest fad in
pop-psychology. Don't preach the latest theological
quirk. Don't be guilty of stealing other men's sermons. You can only preach with authority when
you are confident of the material, and if your confidence is in another man so much that you constantly borrow his material, your confidence won't
be in the Word.

Show your confidence in God's Word by preaching the Word. How are the people ever going to have confidence in God's Word if their minister doesn't? Why should they turn to it for answers when their leaders don't? They will develop a greater confidence in the Word when it is preached with conviction and authority! May God once again raise up a generation of godly preachers who will declare His Word with all the authority that is inherent in it because of its Author.

Evangelistic Preaching

Eric Alexander

As we approach the subject of evangelistic preaching, I think it is important to clarify several issues which lie close to our theme.

The first is a corollary of our basic belief in the authority and sufficiency of the whole Word of God. That implies that the whole Bible has saving and sanctifying power, and therefore we should not really be surprised when people are truly converted when we are preaching on some part of the Bible that we would not readily categorize as "evangelistic" material. We need regularly to relearn Paul's great statement found in 2 Timothy 3:16 that "all Scripture is God-breathed and profitable." My friend and mentor, the Rev. William Still of Aberdeen, used to tell how a lady came to his vestry before the evening service one Sunday to tell him that her niece was with her, and she wanted her to be converted. "That means you will have to preach the gospel tonight!" she added, and flounced out of the room. William Still happened to be preaching through Romans 9-11 at that time, and was not inclined to be diverted. As the aunt seethed with anger in her pew at this "lecture on the Jews," as she chose to describe it, the niece was being converted alongside her.

The lesson from that is not that the next time you are called upon to preach on an "evangelistic occasion" you should necessarily turn to Romans 9–11. The lesson is rather that wherever you are preaching from in the Word of God, you need to remind yourself that God is pleased to use His whole Word toward the salvation of sinners.

The second issue which must constantly be before us in evangelistic preaching is closely related to the first. It is that salvation is the work of God the Holy Spirit. It is so easy for us to slip into that thinking which says, "If I just arrange an evangelistic service, and emphasize certain basic truths from the Bible in my preaching, that will be the means of bringing people to faith in Christ."

It is of paramount importance here, and in every other sphere of our ministry, to recognize that salvation is the sovereign work of God. Left to ourselves, there are many things of which we are capable: we can persuade people intellectually; we can arouse and inspire them emotionally; and we can win them to ourselves psychologically. But the one thing we cannot do is to regenerate them spiritually. That is a task which is exclusively God's. So when one of my friends, who had been in the pastorate for many fruitful years, was asked by some

seminary students, "What, in your experience, is
the best and most effective evangelistic method?" he
replied after some thought, "Prayer—persistent, believing prayer." Now, if you think about it, that reply does not derive from some profound theological
insight. It derives from basic, logical thinking. If
only God can save, then to whom do we turn to see
our friends brought to salvation? The logical answer is, "To God!" The awkward question which
follows that is, "Then why is it that most ministries
and in most churches, prayer is supplemental
rather than fundamental?" That is the background
against which we need to think about evangelistic
preaching.

At this point, I want us to turn to Paul's second
letter to the Corinthians, chapter 5:11–21:

> Since then we know what it is to fear the Lord,
> we try to persuade men. What we are is plain
> to God, and I hope it is also plain to your con-
> science. We are not trying to commend our-
> selves to you again, but are giving you an op-
> portunity to take pride in us so that you can
> answer those who take pride in what is seen,
> rather than in what is in the heart. If we are
> out of our mind, it is for the sake of God. If we
> are in our right mind, it is for you. For
> Christ's love compels us, because we are con-
> vinced that One died for all, and therefore all
> died. And He died for all so that those who live

shall no longer live for themselves, but for Him who died for them and was raised again. So from now on we regard no one from a worldly point of view; though we once regarded Christ in this way, we do so no longer. Therefore, if anyone is in Christ, He is a new creation. The old has gone. The new has come. All this is from God, who reconciled us to Himself through Christ and gave us the ministry of reconciliation, that God was reconciling the world to Himself in Christ, not counting men's sins against them. And He has committed to us the message of reconciliation. We are, therefore, Christ's ambassadors, as though God were making His appeal through us. We implore you, on Christ's behalf, be reconciled to God. God made Him who had no sin to be sin for us, so that in Him we might become the righteousness of God.

Second Corinthians is often thought to be one of the Apostle Paul's most personal letters. He has clearly been under some great pastoral and personal stress. He has been the object of some serious criticism regarding his integrity, his true motivation in preaching the gospel, and even the soundness of his mind!

It should not surprise us, therefore, that in the first few verses of this passage, Paul is defending his integrity and clarifying his motives as a preacher of the gospel. In verse 9, he sets down the

ultimate goal which directs both his life and his
work: "We make it our goal to please Him." Then,
in verses 11 and 14, he explains what the motivation of his preaching is: in verse 11 it is the fear of
God; in verse 14 it is the love of Christ.

MOTIVE 1: The Fear of God. Of course the fear of
the Lord is just the proper reaction of sinners to
God's infinite holiness, or of creatures to God's infinite majesty. As we grow in the knowledge of
God, we will learn truly to tremble before His great
glory and burning purity, and see this as indeed
the beginning of wisdom. Paul is, of course, referring to his own appearance before the judgment
seat (verse 10), as well as to the appearance of the
Corinthians there. His great burden for unbelievers
is that they may not come to this great and awesome day and find themselves unprepared and in
utter confusion.

Now, notice what impending judgment and the
fear of the Lord do for Paul's evangelism. He does
not say, "Since we know what it is to fear the Lord,
we frighten men." Rather he says, "Since we know
what it is to fear the Lord, we try to persuade men."
Luke uses the same language when he describes
Paul's visit to Corinth in Acts 18:4: "Every Sabbath
he reasoned in the synagogue, trying to persuade
Jews and Greeks."

There is a very important principle for gospel

preaching in Paul's and Luke's vocabulary. The old order of sin makes its approach and appeal through the appetite (think of the fruit of the tree in the garden which appealed to the eyes and the appetite), whereas the new order of grace makes its appeal through the mind (think of God appealing to the people at the beginning of Isaiah: "Come, now, let us reason together," says the Lord). Confirmation of this principle comes in the language Luke uses to describe the apostolic preaching in Acts. It includes words like *didaschein* (teach), *dialegesthai* (argue), *paratithemi* (prove), and *syzetein* (dispute). Correspondingly, when people are converted they are often said to be "persuaded." Now this does not mean that apostolic evangelism sought a mere intellectual conquest. The ultimate aim was that men and women might repent, believe, and surrender to the lordship of Jesus Christ over the whole of life. But the *approach* is through the mind. As John Stott puts it tersely, "There is no doubt that the early apostolic *kerygma* was full of solid *didache*."*

MOTIVE 2: The Love of Christ. In 2 Corinthians 5:14, Paul comes to the second main motive of his evangelistic preaching: "Christ's love compels us." It is, I think, beyond doubt that Paul is not referring to their love for Christ, but to Christ's love for

---

* J. R. W. Stott. *The Preacher's Portrait* (London: Tyndale Press, 1961), 49.

them. That love has brought them under a compulsion, or a constraint which (in one version) "leaves us no option." The word does not so much have the idea of "driving out" as "hedging around" or "holding in." The best illustration of it I have ever heard came from the Rev. Alan Stibbs, onetime lecturer in New Testament at Oakhill College. He had been a missionary with the China Inland Mission and described to us the course of the River Yangtze at one point in its journey. Apparently on either bank there were high, solid rocks which "constrained" the river in three ways. They gave it unusual depth, since the flow of the water was held in and dug deeply into the river bed. They also gave it drive, and today it produces hydro-electric power. And it gave the river direction. It was held on course. As Stibbs pointed out to us, few eras like our own have so badly needed depth, drive, and direction in the church's life, and the motivation provided by the love of Christ did precisely that for the Apostle Paul.

It would be important to notice, however, that there is nothing vague or general in Paul's reference to the love of Christ. Verse 14 makes it clear that this is the love of Christ as uniquely seen in the death of Christ, and indeed in a particular understanding of His death: "Christ's love compels us because we are convinced that one died for all."

The apostolic understanding of the death of Christ is that it includes at least these three elements: it is substitutionary in its nature (one died for all, that is, in place of all); it is penal in its character (see verse 21, which is a reference to the punishment of the sin of one being transferred to another in the world of Old Testament sacrifices); it is effectual in its achievement (read verse 14: "For Christ's love compels us, because we are convinced that one died for all, and therefore all died." That is, all those for whom He died, died in Him). The sense in which Christ is the substitute for sinners is that He is an effective substitute. By His death in our place He actually achieved our salvation. Finally, Christ's death is revolutionary in its outcome (read verse 15). By our union with Jesus Christ, we die in His death to all that belongs to our past life, and we are raised with Him into a new life. So we cease living unto ourselves, and live instead for Him who died for us and was raised again. That is why Paul is able to say in verse 17 that "if anyone is in Christ, he is a new creation."

Paul's evangelistic preaching in 2 Corinthians 5 illustrates His use of a number of metaphors which are familiar to readers of the Epistles. They are all "picture words" drawn from various spheres of life, and they help us to understand the meaning of Christ's death. Sometimes he uses the language of the law court, like "justification." There the problem is the guilt and condemnation man discovers when He is brought before God as his Judge. What Christ achieves for him by His death is a reversal of the verdict of "guilty," and the assurance that "there is therefore now no condemnation to those who are in Christ Jesus" (Romans 8:1).

Sometimes Paul borrows from the commercial world, with the language of "redemption," which carries the idea of a slave in the slave market, bound in chains and waiting for someone to pay the price of liberation. Christ is then the One who pays our ransom price and we are redeemed by His blood, that is, by His death.

Here in 2 Corinthians 5, Paul uses a much more familiar metaphor than any of the others. It is the metaphor of reconciliation, behind which there lies the idea of man being separated and alienated from God. We use this widely today of alienation in the domestic and personal world, the national and international world, the world of racial separation and industrial alienation. In all these spheres the great need we recognize is for reconciliation. But Paul is persuading us that the ultimate alienation is not between man and man, or between one race and another, or between one group of society and another, but between man and God. This is the ultimate human tragedy: we are, by our sinful nature, alienated from God. The miracle of the gospel is that God reconciles us to Himself through Jesus Christ by making our sin Christ's and by making His righteousness ours. That is what Paul is referring to in verse 21: "God made Him who had no sin to be sin for us, so that in Him we might become the righteousness of God." There is the glorious work of reconciliation which God has achieved through Christ. It is His work and His alone (verse 18). Archbishop Temple once said, "The only thing of our very own which we contribute to our salvation is the sin which makes it necessary."

But in verse 18 Paul speaks not only of the gift of salvation God gives us in Christ; he speaks also of the gift of a ministry of reconciliation which involves us in carrying to the world the message of reconciliation (verse 19). It is to this task that Paul gives the lofty title of "Christ's ambassadors." The privilege of this ministry is multiplied when we realize that whereas God achieved the reconciliation through Christ (verse 18), He appeals to men and women through us (verse 20). Just as Christ is the Agent for procuring the reconciliation, we are the agents for proclaiming it: "We are therefore Christ's ambassadors, as though God were making His appeal through us. We implore you on Christ's behalf: be reconciled to God."

It is one of the great mysteries of the universe that when God was planning the salvation of His people, He chose Christ to be the Agent for obtaining that salvation through His death, and He also chose faithful preachers of His gospel to be the agents for pleading with sinners to receive that salvation. What an amazing calling! What an incredible privilege!

Finally, let me set out five permanent principles for evangelistic preaching we need to guide us:

1. The Word of God, which we have in Holy Scripture, is our only infallible authority for the substance of the message of the gospel.

2. The gospel's theme is Jesus Christ as the only Savior of sinners (cf. Peter's preaching in Acts 2).

3. The Christ who saves is the Christ who is revealed to us in the whole of Scripture. We should therefore find the Holy Spirit convicting and saving sinners through the message of the whole Bible. This is precisely the example Jesus Himself gives us in Luke 24:27, on the road to Emmaus and in Jerusalem: "Beginning with Moses and all the prophets, He explained to them what was said in all the Scriptures concerning Himself."

4. The Bible does not save us. It is Christ who saves us. But the only Christ who saves is the Christ who is revealed in the Bible.

in it, as is apparent from the passage we have been studying. One is proclamation ("God was in Christ reconciling the world to Himself"). The other is appeal ("as though God were making His appeal through us"). As John Stott points out in *The Preacher's Portrait*, pages 48-50, there must be no proclamation without appeal, nor appeal without proclamation.

Now my suspicion is that while most of us would be confident that we know what the proclamation involves, we may be less clear about the nature of the appeal. This is partly because the word has become associated with a procedure seen in crusades and missions in many parts of the world. Whatever we may think of that kind of public "going forward," it is certainly not what Paul is referring to. What he is speaking about is an appeal to the heart and conscience of his hearers to receive by repentance and faith the riches of God's saving grace in Jesus Christ. We need to press upon our hearers the necessity of heeding that appeal.

It will be part of the theological conviction of most of us that both repentance and faith are gifts of God. But God does not repent *for* us, nor does He believe *for* us. He implores us and earnestly appeals to us to believe on the Lord Jesus Christ. And it is the sinner who exercises saving faith,

And it is the sinner who exercises saving faith, having been enabled to believe by God.

Unless I am much mistaken, it is this pleading, imploring note which is lacking among those of us who are called to be preachers of the gospel in the 21st century.

May God raise up in our generation a great company of men "constrained by the love of Christ," who will be biblical, Christ-centered, Spirit-anointed ambassadors for Christ, who will combine a single-minded zeal for the glory of God with an earnest longing for the salvation of the lost.

Preaching to Suffering People

John Piper

I begin with five assumptions. Without them, what I have to say about preaching and suffering will not stand.

1. Preaching is expository exultation.
2. Preaching is a normative event in the gathered church.
3. The aim of preaching is the glory of God through Jesus Christ.
4. God is most glorified in our people when our people are most satisfied in Him.
5. Suffering is a universal human experience, designed by God for His glory, but endangering every Christian's faith.

If the aim of preaching is the glory of God through Jesus Christ, and if God is most glorified in our people when they are most satisfied in Him, and if the universal human experience of suffering threatens to undermine their faith in the goodness of God, and thus their satisfaction in His glory, then preaching must aim, week in and week out, to help our people be satisfied in God while suffering.

Indeed, we must help them count suffering as part of why they should be satisfied in God.

We must build into their minds and hearts a vision of God and His ways that help them see suffering not merely as a threat to their satisfaction in God (which it is), but also as a means to their satisfaction in God (which it is). We must preach so as to make suffering seem normal and purposeful, and not surprising in this fallen age. The forces of American culture are almost all designed to build the opposite worldview into our people's minds. Maximize comfort, ease, and security. Avoid all choices that might bring discomfort, trouble, difficulty, pain, or suffering. Add this cultural force to our natural desire for immediate gratification and fleeting pleasures, and the combined power to undermine the superior satisfaction of the soul in the glory of God through suffering is huge.

If we would see God honored in the lives of our people as the supreme value, highest treasure, and deepest satisfaction of their lives, then we must strive with all our might to show the meaning of suffering, and help them see the wisdom and power and goodness of God behind it ordaining; above it governing; beneath it sustaining; and before it preparing. This is the hardest work in the world—to change the minds and hearts of fallen human beings, and make God so precious to them that they count it all joy when trials come, and exult in their afflictions, and rejoice in the plundering of their property, and say in the end, "To die is gain."

This is why preaching is not mere communication and why "communication theory" and getting scholarly degrees in "communication" are so far from the essence of what preaching is about. Preaching is about doing the impossible: making the rich young ruler fall out of love with his comfortable lifestyle and into love with the King of kings so that he "joyfully" sells all that he has to gain that treasure (Matthew 13:44). Jesus said very simply, "With man this is impossible" (Matthew 19:26). The aim of preaching is impossible. No techniques will make it succeed. "But with God all things are possible."

In no place does this become more clear than when preaching confronts suffering. How shall we accomplish the great end of preaching in the face of suffering? Coming to Christ means more suffering, not less, in this world. I am persuaded that suffering is normal and not exceptional. We all will suffer; we all must suffer; and most American Christians are not prepared in mind or heart to believe or experience this. Therefore the glory of God, the honor of Christ, the stability of the church, and the strength of commitment to world missions are at stake. If preaching does not help our people be satisfied in God through suffering, then God will not be glorified, Christ will not be honored, the church will be a weakling in an escapist world of ease, and the completion of the Great Commission with its demand for martyrdom will fail.

There is a certainty of suffering that will come to people if they embrace the Savior. "Teacher, I will follow You wherever You go." Really? "The foxes have holes and the birds of the air have nests, but the Son of Man has nowhere to lay His head" (Matthew 8:19–20). "Many are the afflictions of the righteous" (Psalm 34:19). "A slave is not greater than his master. If they persecuted Me, they will also persecute you" (John 15:20). "If they have called the head of the house 'Beelzebul,' how much more will they malign the members of his household!" (Matthew 10:25). "Christ also suffered for you, leaving you an example for you to follow in His steps" (1 Peter 2:21). "Do not be surprised at the fiery ordeal among you, which comes upon you for your testing, as though some strange thing were happening to you" (1 Peter 4:12). "Through many tribulations we must enter the kingdom of God" (Acts 14:22). "Let no one be disturbed by these afflictions; for you yourselves know that we have been destined for this" (1 Thessalonians 3:3). We are "fellow heirs with Christ, if indeed we suffer with

Him so that we may also be glorified with Him. For I consider that the sufferings of this present time are not worthy to be compared with the glory that is to be revealed to us" (Romans 8:17–18). "All who desire to live godly in Christ Jesus will be persecuted" (2 Timothy 3:12). "I protest, brethren, by my pride in you which I have in Christ Jesus our Lord, I die every day!" (1 Corinthians 15:31 RSV). "If for this life only we have hoped in Christ, we are of all men most to be pitied" (1 Corinthians 15:19 RSV). People are going to suffer—that is certain.

And when this life of necessary suffering is at an end, there remains the last enemy, death. "It is appointed for men to die once and after this comes judgment" (Hebrews 9:27). For God's loved ones, dying will be the final suffering. For most of us it will be a terrible thing. In more than twenty years in the pastorate, I have walked with many saints through the last months and days and hours of dying. And very few have been easy. Everyone I preach to is going to die if Christ delays His coming. All must suffer and all must die.

"You sweep them away as with a flood; they are like a dream, like grass. . . . In the morning it flourishes and is renewed; in the evening it fades and withers. The years of our life are seventy, or even by reason of strength eighty; yet their span is but toil and trouble; they are soon gone, and we fly away. . . . So teach us to number our days that we may get a heart of wisdom" (Psalm 90:5–12, ESV).

What does a pastoral heart of wisdom do when it discovers that death is sure, that life is short, and that suffering is inevitable and necessary? The answer is given two verses later in Psalm 90. It is a prayer: "Have pity on Your servants! Satisfy us in the morning with Your steadfast love, that we may rejoice and be glad all our days" (verses 13b–14, ESV). In the face of toil and trouble and suffering and death, the wise preacher cries out with the psalmist, "Satisfy us in the morning with Your steadfast love." He prays this both for himself and for his people: "O God, grant that we would be satisfied with Your steadfast love always, and need nothing else"—and then he preaches to that end.

Why? Because if a preacher leaves his people where they are, seeking satisfaction in family and job and leisure and toys and sex and money and food and power and esteem, when suffering and death strip it all away they will be embittered and angry and depressed. And the worth and beauty and goodness and power and wisdom of God, the glory of God, will vanish in the cloud of murmuring, complaining, and cursing.

But if the preacher has prayed well (that God would satisfy them with Himself); if the preacher has preached well (showing them that they must suffer, but that God is more to be desired than comfort and the steadfast love of the Lord is better than life (Psalm 63:3); if the preacher has lived well (rejoicing to suffer for their sake); and if the preacher has lingered long enough in one place of ministry, then many of the people will suffer well and die well, counting it gain because they are satisfied in God alone. God will therefore be mightily glorified, and the great end of preaching will be achieved.

Preaching and the Suffering of the Preacher

If the ultimate aim of preaching is the glory of God through Jesus Christ, if God is most glorified when we are most satisfied in Him, and if suffering threatens that satisfaction and must come, then we should preach so as to help our people say with the psalmist, from their heart, "The steadfast love of the Lord is better than life" (Psalm 63:3), and to say with Paul, "I count everything as loss because of the surpassing worth of knowing Christ Jesus my Lord" (Philippians 3:8, RSV). Preachers must have a passion to produce people whose satisfaction in God is so solid, so deep, and so unshakable that suffering and death—losing everything this world can give—will not make people murmur or curse God, but rest in the promise, "In His presence is fullness of joy, at His right hand are pleasures forevermore" (Psalm 16:11).

But how shall men preach like that? The answer is that the preacher must suffer and the preacher must rejoice. The preacher himself must be hurt in the ministry, and the preacher must be happy in God.

Follow with me the three generations of preaching from Christ through the Apostle Paul to Timothy. Jesus Christ came into the world to suffer. He took on human flesh so that there would be a body to torture and kill (Hebrews 2:14). Suffering was the heart of His ministry. "The Son of Man did not come to be served, but to serve, and to give His life a ransom for many" (Mark 10:45). "Though He was rich, yet for your sake He became poor so that you, through His poverty, might become rich" (2 Corinthians 8:9). "Thus it is written, that the Christ should suffer and on the third day rise from the dead" (Luke 24:46, RSV). "And He began to teach them that the Son of Man must suffer many things and be rejected by the elders and the chief priests and the scribes, and be killed, and after three days rise again" (Mark 8:31). When Jesus preached, He preached as one whose suffering embodied His message. He is absolutely unique in this. His suffering was the salvation that he preached.

But even though He was unique (and a

preacher's suffering will never be the salvation of people in the same way), nevertheless He calls us to join Him in this suffering. Christ then makes that suffering part of our ministry and, in great measure, the power of our message. When they wanted to follow Him He said, "The foxes have holes and the birds of the air have nests, but the Son of Man has nowhere to lay His head" (Matthew 8:19–20). In other words, "Do you really want to follow Me? Know what you were called to!" "A slave is not greater than his master. If they persecuted Me, they will also persecute you" (John 15:20). "If they have called the head of the house Beelzebul, how much more will they malign the members of his household!" (Matthew 10:25). "As the Father has sent Me, even so I send you" (John 20:21, RSV). Or, as Peter put it, "Christ also suffered for you, leaving you an example for you to follow in His steps" (1 Peter 2:21).

Specifically concerning the Apostle Paul, the risen Christ said, "I will show him how much he must suffer for My name's sake" (Acts 9:16). Paul understood his own sufferings as a necessary extension of Christ's for the sake of the church. So he said to the Colossians, "I rejoice in my sufferings for your sake, and in my flesh I complete what is lacking in Christ's afflictions for the sake of His body, that is, the church" (Colossians 1:24, RSV).

His sufferings did not complete the atoning worth of Christ's sufferings. You can't complete perfection. They completed, rather, the extension of those sufferings in person, in a suffering representative, to those for whom Christ suffered.

Paul had to suffer in the ministry of the gospel. It was an essential extension of the sufferings of Christ. Why? Besides extending the sufferings of Christ in Paul's own suffering to others, there are other reasons. One of his testimonies gives another answer: "For we do not want you to be unaware, brethren, of our affliction which came to us in Asia, that we were burdened excessively, beyond our strength, so that we despaired even of life; indeed, we had the sentence of death within ourselves so that we would not trust in ourselves, but in God who raises the dead" (2 Corinthians 1:8–9). Notice the purpose of this suffering: "So that we would not trust in ourselves, but in God who raises the dead." This is not the purpose of Satan, and it is not the purpose of Paul's enemies. It is the purpose of God. God ordained the suffering of His apostle so that he would be radically and totally dependent on nothing else but God. All is about to be lost on this earth. If there is anything left to hope in, it is God alone, who raises the dead. That is all. Paul's sufferings are designed to throw him back again and again on God alone as his hope and treasure.

But that is not the end of God's purpose.
2 Corinthians 1:8–9 begins with the word "for."
Paul's sufferings are meant to support what goes
before, namely, the comfort of the church. Paul says
this several ways. For example, verse 6: "If we are
afflicted, it is for your comfort and salvation; or if
we are comforted, it is for your comfort." So Paul's
affliction as a minister of the Word is designed not
only to throw him solely on God for his comfort,
but also to bring that same comfort and salvation
to the people he serves. His suffering is for their
sake.

How does that work? How do Paul's sufferings
help his people find their comfort and satisfaction
in God alone? Paul explains it like this: "We have
this treasure [the treasure of the gospel of the glory
of Christ] in earthen vessels, so that the surpassing
greatness of the power will be of God and not from
ourselves; we are afflicted in every way, but not
crushed; perplexed, but not despairing; persecuted,
but not forsaken; struck down, but not destroyed"
(2 Corinthians 4:7–9). In other words, these terrible
things happen to Paul to show that the power of
his ministry is not from himself, but is God's
power (verse 7). Paul's suffering is designed by God
to magnify the "surpassing greatness" of God's
power.

He says it again in verse 10: "Always carrying

about in the body the dying of Jesus, so that the life of Jesus also may be manifested in our body." In other words, Paul shares in the sufferings of Christ in order to display the life of Jesus more clearly. The aim of the ministry of the preacher is to display Christ, to show that He is more to be desired than all earthly comforts and pleasures. And the suffering of the preacher is designed to make clear that Christ is in fact that valuable, that precious. "I die daily," he says, "so that the surpassing value of Christ will be seen in my suffering body." This is how it works. This is how Paul's sufferings help his people find their comfort and satisfaction in God alone.

Paul says it again in 2 Corinthians 12:9. When he implored the Lord to take away the painful thorn in the flesh, Christ answered: "My grace is sufficient for you, for power is perfected in weakness." And Paul responds, "Most gladly, therefore, I will rather boast about my weaknesses, so that the power of Christ may dwell in me. Therefore I am well content with weaknesses, with insults, with distresses, with persecutions, with difficulties, for Christ's sake; for when I am weak, then I am strong." Paul's thorn in the flesh was to humble Paul and magnify the all-sufficiency of the grace of Christ.

So the suffering of the apostle displays the

"surpassing greatness" of the power of God (2 Corinthians 4:7), the triumph of the "life of Jesus" (2 Corinthians 4:10), and the perfection of "the grace of Christ" (2 Corinthians 12:9). And when the people see this in the suffering of the Apostle Paul, it causes them to treasure Christ as more precious than life, which produces a radically transformed life to the glory of God.

Paul explains this dynamic in 2 Corinthians 3:18: "And we all, with unveiled face, beholding the glory of the Lord, are being changed into His likeness from one degree of glory to another" (RSV). Beholding is becoming. When we see Him for who He really is in His glory, our hearts cherish Him, and thus magnify Him, and we are changed. Everything changes. That is the goal of preaching. And that is the goal of the suffering of the preacher.

Paul puts it in one cryptic sentence in 2 Corinthians 4:12: "Death works in us, but life in you." Suffering, weakness, calamity, and hardship work death in Paul, and in so doing show that the surpassing greatness of his ministry belongs to Christ, not to him. And that manifestation of the surpassing worth of Christ works life in those who see, because life comes from seeing and savoring Christ as our highest treasure.

So Christ comes to preach and to suffer. His suffering and death are the heart of His message.

Then He appears to Paul and tells him how much he must suffer in the ministry of the gospel—not because Paul's suffering and death is the content of his message, Christ's is. But because, in his suffering, Christ's suffering is seen and presented to those for whom He suffered, and His glory shines with surpassing value as the greatest treasure of the universe.

Then, when Paul undertakes to help Timothy (and us), what does he say? He says, by way of example, in 2 Timothy 2:10, "I endure everything for the sake of the elect, that they also may obtain salvation in Christ Jesus with its eternal glory" (RSV). God's assignment for him as a minister of the Word is to suffer for the elect.

Then he turns to Timothy and gives him the same calling, which is why I believe it applies to us. "Timothy, making disciples will cost you dearly." 2 Timothy 2:2–3: "The things which you have heard from me in the presence of many witnesses, entrust these to faithful men who will be able to teach others also. Suffer hardship with me, as a good soldier of Christ Jesus." Entrust the word to others, Timothy. The price: "Suffer hardship with me."

But what about preaching in particular? Paul addresses the issue directly in 2 Timothy 4:2–5: "Preach the Word; be ready in season and out of season; reprove, rebuke, exhort, with great patience and instruction. For the time will come when they will not endure sound doctrine; but wanting to have their ears tickled, they will accumulate for themselves teachers in accordance to their own desires, and will turn away their ears from the truth and will turn aside to myths. But you, be sober in all things, endure hardship." Preach the word, endure hardship! Preach the Word, Timothy. The price? Endure hardship.

We must preach with a passion to produce people whose satisfaction in God is so solid, so deep, and so unshakable that suffering and death will not make our people murmur or curse God, but will help them count it all joy (James 1:2) and say with Paul, "To live is Christ and to die is gain" (Philippians 1:21). How will that happen? I said that the preacher must suffer. That is what I have tried to show thus far. And then the preacher must rejoice. He must be hurt in the ministry, and he must be happy in God.

Of course Paul commands this of all of us. "Rejoice in the Lord always; again I say, rejoice" (Philippians 4:4). "We exult in hope of the glory of God. And not only this, but we also exult in our tribulations" (Romans 5:2–3). It is crucial to see how Paul speaks of his own experience in suffering in the ministry of the Word. He does not just say to the Colossians, "I suffer for your sake." He says, "I rejoice in my sufferings for your sake." He doesn't just say to the Corinthians, "I boast about my weaknesses." He says, "Most gladly, therefore, will I boast about my weaknesses" (2 Corinthians 12:9). Yes, there is sorrow, sometimes almost unbearable sorrow. But even here he says, "as sorrowful, yet always rejoicing" (2 Corinthians 6:10). And when he writes to the Thessalonians to commend them for their faith, he says, "You also became imitators of us and of the Lord, having received the Word in much tribulation with the joy of the Holy Spirit" (1 Thessalonians 1:6).

Why this stress on joy in the Lord, joy in the hope of the glory of God, joy from the Holy Spirit, and all in the midst of suffering? The reason is this: The aim of preaching is the glory of God through Jesus Christ. God is most glorified in us when we are most satisfied in Him. But suffering is a great threat to our satisfaction in God. We are tempted to murmur, complain, blame, and even to curse and quit the ministry. Therefore, joy in God in the midst of suffering makes the worth of God— the all-satisfying glory of God—shine more brightly than it would through our joy at any other time. Sunshine happiness signals the value of sunshine. But happiness in suffering signals the value of God. Suffering and hardship joyfully accepted in

the path of obedience to Christ show the suprema-
cy of Christ more than all our faithfulness in fair
days.

When a preacher preaches with this joy and
this suffering, the people will see Christ for the infinite value that He is, and, seeing, will cherish
Him above all things and thus be changed from
one degree of glory to the next. The glory of God
will be magnified in the church and in the world,
and the great aim of preaching will be achieved.

Preaching and the Suffering of the People

Suffering will come to believers. It must come. It
is part of their calling. In Philippians 1:29, Paul
tells the entire church in Philippi, "To you it has
been granted for Christ's sake not only to believe in
Him, but also to suffer for His sake." This is a gift
from God to all believers. We are appointed to suffer. "You yourselves know that we have been destined for this" (1 Thessalonians 3:3). We are
preaching to disciples of Jesus, not disciples of
Hugh Hefner. "Can we wish, if it were possible, to
walk in a path strewed with flowers when His was
strewed with thorns?"[1]

For the glory of God to be manifest in our people's lives, they must rejoice in suffering rather

---

[1] John Newton, *The Works of John Newton,* vol. 1 (Edinburgh: The Banner
of Truth Trust, 1985), 230.

than murmur and complain. This is why the Bible tells them again and again, "Blessed are you when men revile you . . . rejoice and be glad" (Matthew 5:11–12, RSV). "We rejoice in our sufferings, knowing that suffering produces endurance" (Romans 5:3, RSV). "Count it all joy . . . when you meet various trials" (James 1:2). "Rejoice in so far as you share Christ's sufferings" (1 Peter 4:13, RSV). "You joyfully accepted the plundering of your property" (Hebrews 10:34, RSV). "They left the presence of the council, rejoicing that they were counted worthy to suffer dishonor for the name" (Acts 5:41, RSV).

People are not prepared or able to rejoice in suffering unless they experience a massive biblical revolution of how they think and feel about the meaning of life. Human nature and American culture make it impossible to rejoice in suffering. This is a miracle in the human soul wrought by God through His Word. It is the aim of preaching to be the agent of God in bringing about that miracle through the Word.

Jesus said to Peter at the end of John's Gospel, " 'When you grow old, you will stretch out your hands and someone else will gird you, and bring you where you do not wish to go.' Now this He said, signifying by what kind of death he would glorify God" (John 21:18–19). In other words, God appoints a kind of suffering and death by which each of us is called to glorify God. And, since the great aim of preaching is the glory of God, we must preach to prepare people to suffer and die like that.

It is important, then, for preachers to understand how their own suffering affects their preaching for the sake of their suffering people.

First, God has ordained that our preaching become deeper and more winsome as we are broken, humbled, and made low and desperately dependent on grace by the trials of our lives. Jesus said it about His own ministry like this: "Come to Me, all who labor and are heavy laden, and I will give you rest. Take My yoke upon you, and learn from Me; for I am gentle and lowly in heart, and you will find rest for your souls" (Matthew 11:28–29, RSV). People will come and learn from us how to suffer if we are "gentle and lowly in heart." And that is what our sufferings are designed to make us. "We were so utterly, unbearably crushed that we despaired of life itself . . . [so that we would] rely not on ourselves but on God who raises the dead" (2 Corinthians 1:8–9, RSV). God aims to break us of all pretenses to self-sufficiency, and make us lowly and childlike in our dependence on God. This is the kind of preacher to whom the suffering come.

John Newton wrote to a fellow pastor and said,

> It belongs to your calling of God as a minister, that you should have a taste of the various

> spiritual trials which are incident to the Lord's
> people, that thereby you may . . . know how
> to speak a word in season to them that are
> weary; and it is likewise needful to keep you
> perpetually attentive to that important admo-
> nition, "Without Me ye can do nothing."[2]

It is true that we must be bold in the pulpit and afraid of no man but courageous as we contend for the truth. But it is just as true that our boldness must be brokenhearted boldness, that our courage must be a contrite and lowly courage, and that we must be tender contenders for the truth. If we are brash and harsh and cocky and clever, we may win a hearing with angry and pugnacious people, but we will drive away those who suffer. Paul makes it so clear that we are laid low and given comfort "so that we will be able to comfort those who are in any affliction with the comfort with which we ourselves are comforted by God" (2 Corinthians 1:4). It must feel to our people that we are utterly dependent in our lives on the merciful comfort of God to make it through our days.

Second, God has ordained that when we preach from weakness and suffering sustained by joy in Christ, the people see that Christ is treasured and they are loved. Here we are up against a huge ob-

---

[2] John Newton, *The Works of John Newton,* vol. 1, 255.

stacle in American culture. The twentieth century was the century of the self. Almost all virtues, especially love, were reinterpreted to put the self at the center. This means that almost all our people are saturated and shaped with the conviction that the essence of being loved as a human is being treasured or esteemed. That is, you love me to the degree that your act of treasuring terminates on me.

But God ordains the suffering of preachers to show the all-surpassing worth of Jesus because we treasure Christ as we preach to our people. And if they ask, "Do you treasure me or do you treasure Christ?" I answer, "I treasure Christ, and, desiring to treasure Him more, I treasure your treasuring Christ." Without the miraculous work of the Holy Spirit removing human self from the center, this will not satisfy American people. They are so saturated with self-oriented love that they can scarcely conceive what true Christian love is. True Christian love is not my making much of them, but my helping them to enjoy making much of God. This is love. If my treasuring terminates on them, I play right into the hands of the devil and their own self-centered destruction. But if my treasuring terminates on God and their treasuring God, then I direct them to the one source of all joy. And that act of directing them to God, their hope and life and joy, is what love is.

Our aim in preaching is not to help our people feel treasured, but to help them treasure God. We must aim to preach in such a way that we breed a kind of people who feel loved not when they are made much of, but when they are patiently helped to enjoy making much of God, even when they themselves are slandered, ridiculed, persecuted, and killed. This is impossible with man, but with God all things are possible. When the Holy Spirit comes in power on our preaching, people see that Christ is treasured and they are loved, and that those two things are one. God has ordained that one way they see Christ treasured in us is how we are sustained by Him in suffering.

Third, the suffering of the preacher helps him see from the Scripture what he must say to his suffering people. Martin Luther made the point powerfully and straight out of the Bible, not just from experience. He cites Psalm 119:67 and 71: "Before I was afflicted I went astray, but now I keep Your word. . . . It is good for me that I was afflicted, that I may learn Your statutes." Here Luther found an indispensable key for the preacher in unlocking texts. "It was good for me that I was afflicted that I may learn Thy statutes." There are things to see in the Word of God that our eyes can only see through the lens of tears.

Luther said it this way: "I want you to know

how to study theology in the right way. I have practiced this method myself. . . . Here you will find three rules. They are frequently proposed throughout Psalm [119] and run thus: *Oratio, meditatio, tentatio* (prayer, meditation, tribulation)."[3] And tribulations he called the "touchstone." They "teach you not only to know and understand, but also to experience how right, how true, how sweet, how lovely, how mighty, how comforting God's Word is; it is wisdom supreme."[4]

He proved the value of suffering over and over again in his own experience. "For as soon as God's Word becomes known through you, the devil will afflict you, will make a real doctor of you, and will teach you by his temptations to seek and to love God's Word. For I myself . . . owe my papists many thanks for so beating, pressing, and frightening me through the devil's raging that they have turned me into a fairly good theologian, driving me to a goal I should never have reached."[5]

Luther calls it theology. I call it preaching. In other words, Psalm 119:71 teaches us that the suffering of the preacher opens to him the Scriptures in a way he would not otherwise know them, and

---

[3] Ewald M. Plass, *What Luther Says,* vol. 3 (St. Louis: Concordia Publishing House, 1959), 1359.
[4] *Ibid.*, 1360.
[5] *Ibid.*

so shows him in the Scriptures what to say to his people, mingled with how to say it.

The first thing you will learn to say to your people is that they must suffer. You will make it a theme running through all your messages: They will get sick; they will be persecuted; and they will die. They must be reminded of these things again and again, because almost all forces in the culture are pushing them away from these realities and trying to get them not to think about it and therefore not to be ready for it, and certainly not to value it when it comes.

When suffering teaches you the meaning of Scripture, you will learn and preach that all suffering is of one piece, and that saints will taste all of it—sickness, persecution, and death.

You will show them from Romans 8:23 that they will get sick. "We ourselves, having the first fruits of the Spirit, even we ourselves groan within ourselves, waiting eagerly for our adoption as sons, the redemption of our body." Yes, you will teach them to pray for their healing, but you will also teach them that the full and final blood-bought healing of Christ is for the age to come when all crying and pain and tears will be no more (Revelation 21:4). In this age we groan, waiting for the redemption of our bodies. Here the outer nature is wasting away while our inner nature is being renewed day by day

(2 Corinthians 4:16). We will preach this and give our people a theology of sickness.

And we will preach that persecution, whether small or large, must come. "Indeed, all who desire to live godly in Christ Jesus will be persecuted" (2 Timothy 3:12). You will balance with warning the caution that they not seek to provoke offense. The gospel and the path of sacrifice and the cause of truth are the offense, not the cranky personalities of the saints. The aim is to treasure Christ above all things, and to love people with the truth no matter the cost. That will bring the trouble. We must preach to motivate them and prepare them.

We will preach that they must all die, and we will bend every effort to help them say, when the time comes, "To die is gain." If we can help them value Christ above all that death will take away, they will be the freest and most radical, sacrificial people in life.

Not only must we preach that people will all get sick and be persecuted and die, but also that God is sovereign and designs all their suffering for their everlasting good. John Newton again is right when he says that one of Satan's main devices against God's people is to hide from them the Lord's designs in permitting him thus to rage.[6] Preaching should not hide these designs, but reveal them.

---

[6] John Newton, *The Works of John Newton*, vol. 1, 233.

That is how we will establish our people and give them hope and joy in suffering. They must know and cherish the truth that their adversaries (natural and supernatural) meant it for evil, but God meant it for good (Genesis 50:20).

Some people will stumble over the word "designs," that God actually plans the suffering of His people and therefore has good designs in it. William Barclay (an old-line liberal from a generation ago) represents many when he says, "I believe that pain and suffering are never the will of God for His children."[7] There are open theists today who teach, "God does not have a specific divine purpose for each and every occurrence of evil."[8] Or, as one says, "When an individual inflicts pain on another individual, I do not think we can go looking for 'the purpose of God' in the event. . . . I know Christians frequently speak about 'the purpose of God' in the midst of a tragedy caused by someone else. . . . But this I regard to simply be a piously confused way of thinking."[9]

Do not preach that to your people and under-

---

[7] William Barclay, *A Spiritual Autobiography* (Grand Rapids, Mich.: William B. Eerdmans Publishing Co., 1975), 44.
[8] John Sanders, *The God Who Risks: A Theology of Providence* (Downers Grove, Ill.: InterVarsity Press, 1998), 262.
[9] Greg Boyd, *Letters from a Skeptic: A Son Wrestles with His Father's Questions about Christianity* (Colorado Springs: Chariot Victor Publishing, 1994), 46–47.

mine their Biblical hope. Their hope is this—and you will see it most clearly and say it most sweetly when you have experienced it most deeply—that all their suffering is the discipline of their Father for their good (Hebrews 12:11); it is the refining fire of faith (1 Peter 1:7); it is the crucible of perseverance and character and hope (Romans 5:3–4); it is the preparation of an eternal weight of glory beyond all comparison (2 Corinthians 4:17). And if they will believe and rejoice, it is the display of the supreme value of Christ when your people say, "The steadfast love of the LORD is better than life" (Psalm 63:3). It is not by accident, but by design, that all wise people confess with Malcolm Muggeridge who, at the end of his life, said, "Looking over my 90 years, I realize I have never made any progress in good times. I only progressed in the hard times."[10] When we experience this, we are more alert to it in Scripture, and when we see it, then we preach it for our suffering people.

There is one last connection between the preacher's suffering and the suffering of his people, namely, that his suffering will show him that the timing of teaching and touching is crucial. "There is a time for everything . . . a time to weep, and a

---

[10] Quoted in Fred Smith, "Mentored by the Prince of Preachers," *Leadership* (Summer 1992), 54.

time to laugh; a time to mourn, and a time to dance; . . . a time to embrace, and a time to refrain from embracing; . . . a time to keep silence, and a time to speak" (Ecclesiastes 3:1, 4–7, RSV). Preaching involves timing. Preach the whole truth about suffering and the sovereign goodness of God while it is day, and when the night comes and you stand beside the suicide victim's pool of blood or the ice-cold, ivory body of a one-year-old boy, you won't have to say anything. This will be a time for embracing. At this point the suffering saints will be glad that your suffering has taught you to preach the hard things and then, at the right time, to be silent.

When you walk through your own valley of darkness you learn these things. This is your life-long seminary. If you are called to preach, I entreat you, do not begrudge the seminary of suffering.

A Reminder to Shepherds

John MacArthur, Jr.*

Years ago a magazine premiered here called *New West*. In the first edition there was an article about Christians on television. There was a line the journalist wrote at the end of his article which I'll never forget: "Personally, I assume Jesus has more class than most of His agents." He was right. Jesus definitely has more class than *all* of His agents. It is an old adage that you can't tell the value of something by the package it comes in. That is certainly true of preachers and of the rest of us who are witnesses to the gospel of Jesus Christ. Like the treasure of salvation buried in the dirt in the parable that Jesus told, the treasure is so precious that the man sold everything to buy it. And like the pearl without price hidden in the ugly oyster shell for which a man gave up everything, the container doesn't always reflect the value of its contents.

That contrast is the heart of 2 Corinthians 4. Often I am asked to sign a Bible or one of my

---

* This chapter is adapted from a message delivered to pastors at Grace Community Church's annual Shepherd's Conference, 2001.

books, and when I do so I put 2 Corinthians 4:5-7
under my name, because this is a passage in which
I find my life and my ministry defined. Verse 5
says, "For we do not preach ourselves, but Christ
Jesus as Lord, and ourselves as your bondservants
for Jesus' sake; for God, who said, 'Light shall
shine out of darkness,' is the One who has shone
in our hearts to give the light of the knowledge of
the glory of God in the face of Christ. But we have
this treasure in earthen vessels, that the surpassing
greatness of the power may be of God and not from
ourselves." Here we see the amazing contrast
between the shining glory of God in the face of
Jesus Christ, and the feeble, imperfect, fragile, ugly
containers by which this glorious gospel is carried
and delivered to people.

Let me here give some background. I don't think
that Paul, when he founded the Corinthian church,
had any idea how much they would break his
heart. First of all, they broke his heart by dragging
into their lives as Christians all the sins that they
had been forgiven for in their justification—so he
wrote the first letter to them pointing out iniquity
after iniquity after iniquity that were characteristics
of their pre-Christian life, and telling them to shed
those things. It wasn't long after he had
unburdened his grieving heart over their sin when
false teachers came into the church and brought

heresy, doctrines of demons. In came, as Paul called them, hypocritical liars espousing demonic doctrine. The first thing they had to do when they came into Corinth was achieve status. They had to gain the ascendancy; they had to become believable; they had to rise to the place where they were recognized as teachers, and in order to do that they had to destroy the people's confidence in their pastor, Paul. They assaulted Paul relentlessly, mercilessly, and consistently; for months and months they attacked him and undermined his credibility and integrity, his apostleship and his message. He was so devastated by this on one occasion that he went for a visit, and when he got there in an effort to straighten things out and call them back to himself (not for his own sake, but for the sake of the truth), a man in the congregation apparently stood up and blasted Paul to the face, and nobody defended Paul, and he left with an absolutely shattered heart. He then sent Titus there with another letter, a letter not included in the New Testament, and through Titus he sent them a message: "Don't abandon me, because if you abandon me you'll abandon the truth."

Titus returned with a good report: the people had responded. But Paul knew the false teachers were still there, and he feared for the future because the people were fickle, and so he wrote 2 Corinthi-

ans. That epistle had to be the hardest thing for a
man like Paul to do, because it is a letter in which
he has to defend himself—and the fact is he knows
he is nothing. He has to defend himself as a
teacher of the truth; he has to defend himself as the
apostle of Jesus Christ; he has to defend himself as
the messenger of God, and yet he knows himself to
be nothing; and this is a masterpiece of a man
walking that fine line. We get a glimpse of how he
does that in 2 Corinthians 4:5–7.

The false apostles were relentless in trying to
discredit Paul. They attacked him in every way they
could. In verse 1 he says, "Since we have this ministry," in which he refers back to chapter 3 on the
New Covenant, "as we received mercy." In other
words, "It is mercy that I even have it; it is mercy
that I'm saved; it is mercy that I am called." It is
similar to "I am what I am by the grace of God"
(1 Corinthians 15:10). He says that we don't lose
heart; we have a lot of reason to lose heart, but we
don't lose heart. This ministry is too glorious, and
in spite of what they are saying to you, we have re-
nounced the things hidden because of shame.
What the false teachers apparently were saying was
that if you really knew Paul you'd know that he is a
hypocrite, a phony, a fake, a deceiver. On the surface, on the outside, he looks religious, he looks
holy, he looks sanctified and pious; but the fact of

the matter is he has a secret life of shame. He is a
hypocrite; underneath he is a wicked man.

"Furthermore," Paul says "We are not walking in
craftiness," in a great and direct answer to the fact
that they were saying, "He is a manipulator, a con
man." The word used in 2:17 is used for a
huckster. He is saying, "I am not!" They are saying
that he has adulterated the Word, and he says , "I
have not adulterated the Word of God, but by
manifestation of truth commended myself to every
man's conscience in the sight of God." He answers
directly the kinds of things that they were saying
about him.

They even went further than to attack his character; they went further than to attack his theology—they even attacked him personally. They used
that old *ad hominem* argument; they tried to destroy
the man himself. And in chapter 10:10 they said
his personal presence is unimpressive, and his
speech is downright contemptible. What were they
talking about? They said that he was ugly and
couldn't communicate. That is really bad! If you're
handsome, even if you can't communicate, people
can just enjoy looking. And if you're ugly but can
communicate, they'll enjoy listening. But if you're
ugly and can't communicate, you've got nothing!
And when you put it all together, they said he was
unskilled in speech (11:6). He alluded in the first

epistle to the fact that they said he gave this simple message over and over again about the cross, never using the wisdom of men, and not weaving together the great themes of philosophy. Apparently he wasn't intellectual or erudite, and he didn't use any of the charm of the charisma or the persona that makes communication effective. It was really an unkind thing, attacking his personal blemishes, his physical defects. Some commentators have suggested that he was a small hunchback with some physical deformities. We know he was aging and scarred. Whatever his shortcomings in looks were—and he was obviously aware of those—whatever his lack might be in personal charm and attractiveness; whatever his limitations might be in oratorical skills; whatever he might not have had in terms of charm, he was aware. He didn't have the personal power it takes, they said; he didn't have the persona; he didn't have the philosophical relevance to step into this culture and meet it where it was and communicate with it.

Notice his response: "What do you want out of a clay pot?" He turned their arguments back on them. He said, "You're right. I agree about my weaknesses. I agree about my inabilities. I'm not going to pick a fight on that. I'm not here to defend myself." Like all noble ministers he was put in a very embarrassing position; he was being criticized by people much more sinful and weak than he, and yet he found it very hard and very painful to defend himself because he knew he was nothing! But at the same time he knew he was nothing, he knew that the New Covenant was everything. The starkness of the contrast is very apparent. Verses 5–6 blaze out at us as if we stepped into the Holy of Holies in the tabernacle the day the glory arrived, or as if we were standing beside Moses in Exodus when he stood on Mt. Sinai and the glory of God was shown to him; or as if we were Peter, James, and John on the Mount of Transfiguration when Jesus pulled back the veil of His flesh, and the Shekinah blazed forth and put them into a temporary coma; as if you were Isaiah in the temple in Isaiah 6 who had a vision of God that crushed him to the ground and made him confess only his sin and unworthiness; as if you were Ezekiel and saw the vision of God and fainted, or as if you were John who saw the glorified Son in Revelation 1 and fell on his face like a dead man. Paul sees the blazing, shining reality that God, in Christ, in the New Covenant, is saving sinners. He sees the blazing glory of God revealed in the face of Jesus Christ, this glorious New Covenant revelation. And then he says in verse 7, "But we have this treasure in earthen vessels." Frail, imperfect, and common that he was, he agreed with their assessments. It never ceased to be a wonder to Paul, till he died, that God would have put such a priceless treasure in such a clay pot. He was dirt–baked hard; that's what a clay pot is. And Paul knew it.

In 1 Timothy 1, Paul wrote, "I thank Christ Jesus our Lord who strengthened me because He considered me faithful enough, putting me into service." He was in shock! He was at the end of his life here, a man in his 60's. "I was a blasphemer. I was a persecutor. I was a violent aggressor. And yet I was shown mercy, and the grace of our Lord was more than abundant. And, I will tell you, it is a trustworthy statement, deserving full acceptance, that Christ Jesus came into the world to save sinners, among whom I am chief." Note that he did not say, "I was," but "I am." He never got over that.

Preachers, ministers, are men—that's all. And men are not perfect, so there is no hope of perfection in the ministry. If God could not use poor instruments and feeble voices, He couldn't make music. Abraham was guilty of duplicity, yet he became the man of faith and the friend of God. Moses was a man of stuttering speech and a quick temper, yet he was the man chosen to make a nation, and to commune with God and receive His law. David was guilty of adultery, conspiracy, murder, and unfaithfulness as a husband and father; but he repented and became a man after God's own heart and the number-one songwriter of all history. We still sing the songs of this "sweet singer of Israel." Elijah ran from Jezebel, asking for euthanasia, but this same Elijah defied Ahab and all the prophets of Baal, and heard the still small voice of God at Horeb. In the presence of the heavenly vision Isaiah said, "I am a man with a dirty mouth; I live among people with dirty mouths. I'm certainly useless to you, O God." But when he had been cleansed he said, "Here am I; send me." And God said, "Go." Peter was another clay pot, the leader, the spokesman of the twelve apostles who denied his Lord with oaths and curses, who even had the audacity to correct the Lord and was restored by the compassion of Jesus in the midst of his disobedience, and was enabled by the power of the Holy Spirit to speak with such force on the day of Pentecost as to be the agenct by which God brought to birth the great pentecostal introduction to the church. John the apostle expected to be praised by Jesus for refusing to allow a man not of their company to cast out demons in the name of Jesus. He and His brother James wanted to call down fire from heaven and burn up a Samaritan village, and, with James again, wanted the chief places in the kingdom and sent their mother to ask for them. Yet John became the beloved disciple; John became the apostle of love; John became the eagle who soared to great heights. John became, I think, the apostle of all apostles who pierced the deepest into the mystery of the incarnation. Are you seeing a pattern?

So it is with Paul. He was under assault unjustly; he was falsely accused; he was battered and hammered. The attacks against him were usually physical, as in Ephesus when he started a riot and had to escape. In 2 Corinthians 11 he lists all of his beatings: five times beaten by the Jews with 39 stripes; three times beaten with rods by the Gentiles; shipwrecked and on and on and on. Beyond that there was the concern for the churches. Beyond that there was the criticism of the false teachers. The Judaizers relentlessly dogged his steps, plotting at every turn to get rid of him. He suffered so greatly that he literally says in the same passage, "I die daily." That wasn't some mystical, spiritual experience; what he meant was, "I get up every morning realizing that this could be the day I die."

He suffered so much, and he suffered at the hand of the people he loved the most. He even said to the Corinthians, "How is it that the more I love you, the less you love me? I don't get it." And yet, as assaulted as he was, he knew that this was commensurate with what he deserved. He said, in fact, "When I am weak, then I am strong."

His defense all the way through is, "You're right; you're right; you're right. I'm weak, I know." He does not argue against their accusations of weakness; rather he affirms them. Yet they are not defects; they are credentials of his authentic apostleship. This little section in 2 Corinthians 4 unfolds for us a magnificent tribute to a humble man. He defends himself not on the basis of natural talent, and not on the basis of human skill or achievement. He just agrees, and he makes a comparison that is magnificent.

"We have this treasure in earthen vessels, in order that [a purpose clause in the Greek] the surpassing greatness of the power may be of God and not from ourselves." That is why God puts the priceless treasure in clay pots, so that no one ever has to ask where the power comes from! In comparison to the glory of the eternal God revealed in the person of Jesus Christ, in comparison to the magnificence of the New Covenant expressed all through chapter 3, in comparison to Christ's shining glory, the preacher is nothing! In chapter 10 Paul said, "I don't get into comparing myself with other preachers. I just start here: 'We have this treasure, this ministry.' What is the ministry?" The ministry is the gospel (v. 4) of the glory of Christ, who is the image of God. The gospel is the treasure. It is the story of God incarnate in Christ re-

deeming sinners, that great shining gospel, and
that is what is described in the wondrous third
chapter where he unfolds the New Covenant. He
says the treasure is the truth; it is the truth that
God is in Christ, bringing good news of salvation.
This is the treasure. And He put it in clay pots.

It is baked dirt, baked clay, which is really
cheap. It is common, breakable, replaceable, and
essentially valueless. If you drop one, it is no big
deal. A clay pot is a clay pot. It is without value,
but it is useful. Clay pots in ancient times were
used for a number of things. Sometimes something
important was in a clay pot, like the Dead Sea
Scrolls. Sometimes they were used to put somewhat valuable things in and bury them in the
ground, but you couldn't leave them there very
long. But in the home they essentially were used
for garbage and waste, to carry out what was un-
mentionable.

In 2 Timothy 2:20, the same word is used, making it clear what we have here: "In a large house
they have a lot of containers, and there are gold
ones and silver ones and there are wood ones and
clay pots. And the gold and silver ones are to
honor, and the wood and earthenware are not less
honor, but to dishonor." They are the unmention-
ables. And then he says in verse 21, if you are ever
going to use any of these things for honor, you've

got to cleanse it because it is defiled. We are talking here about dishonorable things in the containers that nobody would ever see. The only value they had was the service they performed.

So we can better understand 2 Corinthians where Paul says, "We have this treasure in a garbage can, a waste bucket." We are common containers for the most humble and most dirty uses; never, ever fit in ourselves to be brought into public. That's how it is in the ministry. Our only value is as containers. It's the treasure that we bring that has the value. That's why the Lord didn't choose many mighty or noble. He has chosen the humble, the base, the common. This is the essence of spiritual service. They accused Paul: "You're weak; you're unimpressive; you're not a good communicator; you're plain; you're common; you're not clever; you're not philosophical; and you're not culturally sensitive." His response was this: "I know; I know. I'm just a pot—but do I have a treasure!"

The New Testament was not written by the elite of Egypt. It was not written by the elite of Greece, or Rome, or even Israel. The greatest scholars in the world at that time were down at Egypt; they were in the greatest library of antiquity at Alexandria. The most distinguished philosophers were at Athens; the most powerful leaders and leaders of men were in Rome; and the religious geniuses were in Israel's temple—and God never used any of them! He just used clay pots. He passed by Herodotus, the historian; He passed by Socrates, the philosopher; He passed by Hippocrates, the father of medicine, and Plato, the philosopher. He passed by Aristotle; Euclid, the mathematician; Archimedes, the father of mechanics; Hipparchus, the astronomer, Cicero the orator, and Virgil, the poet. He passed them all. Why? Well, He was looking for clay pots. In their minds, and from a human viewpoint, those people were magnificent vessels, and they were so impressed with their own value they saw no value in the gospel. We have peasants and fishermen, smelly guys, and tax collectors, clay pots, who were chosen to hold and to proclaim and to write the priceless treasure of gospel truth.

God is still doing it that way. He is still passing by the elite. He is still passing by the hard-hearted, non-listening, proud intellectuals. They may be sitting in their ivory towers in the universities, and sitting in their ivory towers in the seminaries, and sitting in their bishoprics and their positions of authority in the church, but God is finding the humble who will carry the treasure of saving truth.

How can that work? Because "we do not preach ourselves." We are not the message. The church where I pastor has been blessed because God has blessed His truth. It's not me. When Paul says,

"When I am weak, then I am strong," he doesn't mean that he is a man with no convictions; he doesn't mean that he is an undisciplined man, a lazy man, an irresponsible man, or a man who can't work and work hard. What he means by weakness is this: "I got myself out of the equation. And that's when the strength became apparent, when I got me out of it."

If you want to be used mightily by God, get yourself out of it. Learn to see yourself as a garbage pail, or, in the words of Peter, clothe yourself with humility. It's not you; it's not your personality; it's the Word of God. He doesn't need the intellectuals. He doesn't need great people, fancy people, or famous people. Because the people aren't the power. The power is the message! "That the surpassing greatness of the power may be of God and not from ourselves."

If you look for a human explanation for Paul's success, there isn't one. People have said to me, "I'm studying the Bible to see why Paul was successful." I'll tell you why he was successful: he preached the truth. And the truth is powerful. Or they will say, "We want to come to your church to find out what makes things tick here." I'll tell you what makes things tick here: the truth of God. The truth of God and the power of God; those are what make things "tick." The surpassing greatness ex-

plains the transcendent might of superlative power
from God on the souls of those who hear the truth.
We preachers are clay pots at best! We have nothing to offer, no beauty or power. Paul knows that,
and he says in 1 Corinthians 1, "I was with you in
weakness, fear and much trembling."

In the end, it's okay that we're so weak and so
afraid. I want to give you God's word, Paul said, so
that your faith would rest in the power of God. In 1
Corinthians 3 he also said, "Neither is the one who
plants anything, or the one who waters is anything.
But God is everything."

Years ago James Denney wrote, "No one who
saw Paul's ministry and looked at a preacher like
Paul could dream that the explanation lay in him.
Not in an ugly little Jew without presence, without
eloquence, without the means to bribe or to compel
could the source of such courage, the cause of such
transformation, be found. It must be sought not in
him, but in God." In 1911, in his book *The Glory of
the Ministry*, A. T. Robertson quoted Denney: "There
always have been men in the world so clever that
God could make no use of them. They could never
do His work; they were so lost in admiration of
their own. God's work never depended on them,
and it doesn't depend on them now. The power is
not the product of human genius, or cleverness, or
technique, or ingenuity; the power of the gospel is

in the gospel." We ministers are weak, common, plain, fragile, breakable, dishonorable, and disposable clay pots who should be taking the garbage out—but instead we're bringing the glory of God to our people.

The amazing thing is that such weakness does not prove fatal to the gospel, because the gospel is not out of us. The great reality is, this is essential to the gospel, because it makes crystal clear where the power really lies. We are unworthy servants, but God has given us the treasure of the gospel. What a privilege!